Enhancing *the* Kingdom

Antonio Crump

ISBN 979-8-89130-994-4 (paperback)
ISBN 979-8-89428-976-2 (hardcover)
ISBN 979-8-89130-995-1 (digital)

Christian Faith Publishing
832 Park Avenue
Meadville, PA 16335
www.christianfaithpublishing.com

All biblical citations were taken from the New King James Version of the Holy Bible.

Printed in the United States of America

CONTENTS

FOREWORD

MY PRAYER FOR the readers of this book is Ephesians 1:18—that the eyes of your understanding be enlightened about the kingdom of God. Faith comes by hearing, and the gospel of the kingdom has not been the gospel we've been taught in the nineteenth and twenty-first centuries. And instead of picking up our own Bibles and studying to show ourselves approved (2 Timothy 2:15), we Christians just leave all the serious studying to the preachers and teachers, and we just live our lives as if going to church from time to time and reading a scripture here and there ought to be good enough to get me to heaven, for God knows my heart.

I would like to remind you that we still have an enemy, and even though Jesus has come and defeated our foe, he's still crafty as always and organized and roams the earth, seeking whom he may devour. The devil is a master at deception and has had many successes. Like in the garden with the first Adam, he was successful in his mission to kill, steal, and destroy. He had no power and no authority on the earth or over man but, through deception, caused man to rebel against God, and man fell and lost his authority to dominate the earth and commune with God. We can do better. In fact, we must do better!

In order to accomplish God's purpose on earth and for our children and children's children, we must create a new norm on earth by obeying the King! We all become part of our culture to an extent—many of the things you might not even recognize until you go to another country or move to another city or state. For example, we used to hear parents make that good old statement: "Do as I say, not as I do." But as they grow up, you will find that they will do what was modeled before them. Yes, you model hitting walls, fussing, drinking, drugs, shutting down, leaving, divorce, or things of that nature when you get mad. They will absolutely take that into their own families as adults, along with whatever issues their partners bring with them but God.

God being who He is—the Alpha and the Omega, the Beginning and the End, the First and the Last—foreknew all things and fixed the problem before the problem existed. God had already had His redemption program before man had eaten the forbidden fruit. Before there was a terminator, there was God. In Genesis 3:15, letting the enemy know—after he had deceived man and stole from him—what God had given to him, *I'll be back*!

Just in case you haven't understood this reality, you don't fight what you create. God had finished redeeming, restoring, and saving His children before He said, "Let there be light." God's Word will not return to Him void, but it will accomplish what He pleases, and it shall prosper in the thing for which He sent it. God, being who He is, always knows the end from the beginning, knowing not only your end (predestined, foreknew) but all-knowing (omniscient) the end. He ended the end before He began!

> *Remember the former things of old, for I am God, and there is no other; I am God, and there is none like Me, Declaring the end from the beginning, and from ancient times things that are not yet done, saying, "My counsel shall stand, and I will do all My pleasure."* (Isaiah 46:9–10)

God's plan and purpose on earth will succeed, but He has left in His Word truths that must be diligently sought out. When you seek Him with your whole heart, He will begin to reveal to you (divine revelation) those mysteries and secrets, revealing those types and shadows of old. But if we live our lives as salvation is enough, then we will not see the promises of God manifest in our lives.

Jesus didn't only come to die for our sins. If so, it wouldn't have taken Him three and a half years of ministry to do so. He finished that in a day. He didn't come to start a religion. He never joined the Pharisees, Sadducees, or the Sanhedrin, but it was them who opposed Him and eventually crucified Him. It was God's representatives on earth who sent Him to the cross. The sinners loved Him. His disciples asked Him, "Why do you speak to them in parables?" See Matthew 13:10–17.

In a nutshell, Jesus said it is given to you (His disciples who had forsaken all to follow Him) to know the mysteries of the kingdom, but to them, it has not been given. It was verse 15 that sums up the answer. Jesus only reveals to you what you want to know. Sala. He says in verse 15, *"For the hearts of the people had grown dull, their ears are hard of hearing, and their eyes they have closed."* They closed their own eyes. They didn't want to know, and Jesus didn't want them to know (see the end of that verse). *"Lest they should understand with their hearts and turn, so that I should heal them."*

John 8:32 says when you know the truth, the truth doesn't set you free, it makes you free. If I had a pet bird in a cage and opened the door to set it free, it could remain in the cage with the door open because its mind is adapted to its confinement. But the truth reaches into the cage and grabs the bird, and outside into the air, he goes, making him free. Religion is not the kingdom (Matthew 23:13)! Jesus rebukes the religious folks in His Olivet discourse, saying, *"Woe to you teachers of the law and Pharisees, you hypocrites!... You shut the door of the kingdom of heaven in people's faces. You yourselves do not enter, nor will you let those enter who are trying to enter."*

Well, if Jesus didn't come to die only and He didn't come to start a religion, why did He come? He came to restore to man what he had lost—the kingdom and man's ability to commune with his heavenly Father. Isaiah 9:6 states, *"For unto us a Child is born, unto us a Son is given, and the Government shall be upon His shoulder."* He brought the government of heaven with Him. That's why He always said the kingdom of heaven is at hand. Repent, for the kingdom of heaven is at hand.

The Greek word for *repent* is *metanoo,* which means "change the way you think."

"For My thoughts are not your thoughts, neither are your ways My ways," declares the Lord. As the heavens are higher than the earth, so are My ways higher than your ways and My thoughts than your thoughts. (Isaiah 55:8–9)

And do not be conformed to this world, but be transformed by the renewing of your mind, that you may prove what is that good and acceptable and perfect will of God. (Romans 12:2)

Religion interprets the word *repent* with the Greek word *metanoeite*, which means "to be sorry." And that's not what Jesus was saying! Be sorry, for the kingdom is at hand. I thought it was supposed to be good news.

I think I'll finish this portion with the definition of *restore* so you can get into these chapters. *Restore* means bring back (a previous right, practice, custom, or situation); reinstate. The second Adam came to *restore* what the first Adam lost! Romans 5:19 says, *"For just as through the disobedience of the one man the many were made sinners, so also through the obedience of the one man the many will be made righteous."*

CHAPTER 1

The Process

Patterns of Life

SINCE THE FALL of man, you see this pattern where man has to grow into what God has purposed him to become or do on earth. For example, Joseph had a dream from God of his family bowing down to him as a man with authority, but when he woke up excited about the dream that the Lord had given him and began to share what God had shown him, his reality didn't look to him like anything he saw in the dream. When he woke up from his dream, he had no authority over his family, and his brothers were quick to let him know. God had given him a dream of his destiny, not the journey or the process. Or how about Moses? Growing up with the Egyptians being educated and raised in their customs, he began to have this feeling that he was to deliver his people from captivity; and in his attempt to do so, he ended up killing a man and becoming Egypt's most wanted.

Instead of delivering his people, he became a fugitive as he found out that his killing the Egyptian was no secret and had to flee Egypt and continue his journey of the process. How about David? When Samuel went to Jessie's house to anoint one of his sons to be king, his father didn't even consider him to be a candidate for such an anointing. David probably didn't comprehend it either, having to grow up in such an environment where you know your father sees you as insignificant just couldn't have been good for his morale. So after he was anointed to be the next king of Israel, he went back outside and tended to his sheep with a king's anointing on him and continued his process.

Now it's easy for us to read about their lives and see the conclusions and say, "God is good or God is faithful," and that He is. Yes, Joseph's dream came true. And yes, Moses delivered God's people. And yes, David became the next king of Israel. But it was many years with many trials and tribulations and tests to come before any of these men saw the will of God manifest in their lives. Let's not forget Israel. God promised Israel a prosperous land where it flowed with milk and honey, and after 430 years of slavery, they began to follow Moses out of captivity into the process. As a nation, they entered the wilderness to be transformed by the renewing of their minds. This is where many Christians live and die—in the wilderness—because they choose to settle. And if that's as far as you are willing to go, then what God has planned for you down the road, you will never know.

You can't lead where you will not go, and you can't preach what you do not know. The journey always comes before destiny. We all will have to go through our personal journeys so that God can make us ready for what He has created us for. He is the author and the finisher of our faith, so no matter what we are going through right now, we have to trust the Lord in His predestined plan for our lives. He did not say everything we go through after salvation will be good, but He did say it will all work together for our good. It is a pattern we all must endure, but we can know that He will never leave us nor forsake us. The trials and tribulations of life are to help us mature spiritually so we can maintain our inheritance when He blesses us with it. He says He will give you beauty for ashes, that is a promise for those who endure to the end.

He says, "Weeping may endure for a night, but joy is coming in the morning." He says, "If you suffer with Me, you will reign with Me." And here is one I know you have heard as well: "Your latter days will be greater than your former days." We need to learn to trust God in our day-to-day walk with Him if we are ever going to see what He had in mind when He created us. I'm sure Israel wonders why after

430 years of slavery, they were not just going straight into this land God promised them after all they had been through. And it was only a forty-day journey from their captivity in Egypt by walking. Exodus 13:17 says, *"Then it came to pass, when Pharaoh had let the people go, that God did not lead them by way of the land of the Philistines, although that was near; for God said, 'lest perhaps the people change their minds when they see war and return to Egypt.'"*

The land God had for them had giants squatting on it with no intent on leaving because it was a productive land; it just flowed with milk and honey. That is not the type of land a man would just walk away from willingly. God had to get them ready to take back what belonged to them.

God's purpose

God loves His children—and not only His children but the world—and not one more than the other. But He knows those that are His. Romans 15:4 says, *"For whatever things were written before were written for our learning, that we through the patience and comfort of the Scriptures might have hope."* God will see to it that His plans and His purpose are done on earth. The sooner we realize that this life we're living is all about Him and how we fit in His scheme of things, the better it will be for us. I heard a quote the other day (not sure from whom) that says, "Without God, we can do nothing. But without man, God will do nothing." We live our lives as Christians as if we forget that God owns us. First Corinthians 6:20 states, *"For you were bought at a price; therefore glorify God in your body and in your spirit, which are God's."*

We are His property living on His earth, in His houses, breathing His air, sleeping in His beds, driving His cars as we enjoy His life. Psalm 24:1 says, "The earth is the Lord's, and all its fullness, the world and those who dwell therein." God owns everything by creative rights, and He can do with it as He pleases. We brought nothing into this world, and we will be taking nothing out when we depart. In other words, He owned it all before you got here, and the stuff you think you own will still be His when you go. In a kingdom, the king owns everything, including the people. That's why it's so important for us to find out His plans and purpose for our lives.

Jesus said in Matthew 10:39, *"Whosoever finds his life will lose it, and whosoever loses his life for My sake will find it."* Before God placed you on the planet, His plans and purpose for you were already awaiting you. We see it in the first and last Adam alone. God created the earth with the garden of Eden already awaiting Adam with all the animals—fish, birds, bugs, trees, plants—and the rest of Adam's responsibilities before Adam even got here. And we know Jesus's assignment awaited Him when He came to earth. Man was lost, the kingdom was lost, the Holy Spirit was gone, and man's mindset was all headed for total destruction.

When God created you, He already had your purpose or His will for your life predestined before he began His creation of you. You were fearfully and wonderfully made. God put the thought into every detail when He was creating you and equipped you with everything necessary for you to succeed in what He purposed for you to do. But instead of us trying to seek God and find out what His plans and purposes are for our lives, we plan our own future, then turn around, and tell God to bless it because we know that this must be what He has in mind for us.

So we pray, "Dear heavenly Father, bless me with a good job, a big house, a Cadillac, so I can be a blessing as I give Your people a ride from here to there, and the Cadillac will bring glory to Your name. And bless me with a spouse because You said, 'It's not good for a man to be alone.' In Jesus's name, I pray. And if you want to be real spiritual, you will throw in and bless our government and Israel too. Amen!"

God knows are motives and intents better than we know our own. Now God does not mind you having things, and He wants you to live a blessed life, but He has much more in mind about you than you do. And we need to learn to seek what that is.

> *For I know the thoughts that I think toward you,*
> *says the Lord, thoughts of peace and not of evil, to*
> *give you a future and a hope. Then you will call*

upon Me and go and pray to Me, and I will listen to you. And you will seek Me and find Me, when you search for Me with all your heart. I will be found by you, says the Lord, and I will bring you back from your captivity; I will gather you from all the nations and from all the places where I have driven you, says the Lord, and I will bring you to the place from which I cause you to be carried away captive.
(Jeremiah 29:11–14)

God knows exactly who you are, where you are, and where He has predestined your life to end up. Your steps are ordered by God. He is not here to do your will, and He is not concerned if you think He is a nice god. Your heavenly Father is King, and we need to get that revelation in our spirit—not a president or a prime minister, but He is a King. Therefore, it behooves us as Christians to know the will of the King for our lives.

Preparation for assignment

When we live our lives believing that it's all about us and God is there to give us whatever our heart desires, as if He's the great Santa Claus in the sky, that type of mindset only lets us know where we are in our development in the work Christ is doing in our lives. He said that He is the author and the finisher of our faith. When you were born again, you were made alive to God again, and the new man you have become has to grow up and mature. Salvation was simply the beginning of a new journey with the Lord that He is well able to perform the work that needs to be done in us to cause us to become what God had in mind for us. So what is the point of all this?

The kingdom of God will only be experienced in its fullness by mature Christians. Christians, whose minds have been renewed, are truly led by the Spirit of God and have grown into the likeness of their heavenly Father. As long as we look like the world, act like the world, and do like the world, we cannot be His witnesses.

*But you shall receive power when the Holy Spirit
has come upon you; and you shall be witnesses to Me
in Jerusalem, and in all Judea, and Samaria, and
to the end of the earth.* (Acts 1:8)

When God says, "You should be my witnesses," what does He mean? Not only to testify with our words but with our lives, being filled with His spirit gives us the power to change and should start bearing fruit or evidence in our natural bodies and behaviors that will testify in itself that we have been changed. When people have any kind of relationship with you, your life should minister to them His existence, His goodness, His love for mankind, His ways, and everything else He reveals to us as His children.

*There is therefore now no condemnation to those
who are in Christ Jesus,* who do not *walk according
to the flesh,* but *according to the Spirit.* (Romans
8:1; emphasis added)

We normally only hear half of that verse quoted. And when it gets to the part where it says, "Who do not walk according to the flesh, but according to the Spirit," it takes too much discipline so we just leave that part out so we can continue to live according to the flesh and pretend that we are blessed. We do not just automatically manifest the fruit of the Spirit because we were filled with the Spirit. We have to submit our lives and obey the Holy Spirit as He leads us, guides us, and reveals the plans and purpose of God concerning our lives to us. If we live our lives in submission to our flesh, we will never inherit the kingdom of God. You might inherit religion, which is no inheritance at all. But we seem to settle for it as if it were because there are so many different religions that there is bound to be a fit for you and your will in one of them somewhere, but not the kingdom. In a kingdom, you must obey the King! Jesus is King. And I, too, like many of my Christian brothers and sisters in the US, have been a citizen of the United States of America my whole life and living with my mind conformed to the culture of a democracy and not a kingdom. We take that mindset to our churches, approach the Word of God, and receive our own private interpretations, which does not persuade the King to change one bit. We just go along with a lot of unanswered prayers and just put a religious spin on why God is not doing what we thought He would do.

When Jesus began His ministry on the earth, the first thing out of His mouth in His public announcement recorded in Matthew 4:17 was, *"Repent, for the kingdom of heaven is at hand."* I showed you in my foreword that the word *repent* means to change the way you think. And *at hand* simply means "is here." So what Jesus said in His opening remarks was, "Change the way you think, for the kingdom of God is here." The gospel of the kingdom is the only thing Jesus preached—not the gospel of grace, the cross, the blood, or redemption but the kingdom. Even after His resurrection, He spent forty days with His disciples, speaking of things about the kingdom of God.

Timing and strategy

It is easy to be distracted from the will of God when your whole relationship is founded on faith—having to live your life disciplined by a God that you cannot see and really don't fully understand His ways and reading His Word that you really don't understand and go to church and hear all these wonderful things that you really don't see manifesting in too many of your new brothers and sisters in Christ. Then everybody tells you that everything is okay because they really don't understand either, not that they would tell you in those words but our lives do minister to people without us saying much with our mouths. What are the benefits for me as a person to serve your God when I'm broke, busted, and disgusted and you're broke, busted, and disgusted? I'm sick, and you're sick. I'm frustrated and depressed, and so are you.

> *Bless the Lord, O my soul; and all that is within me,*
> *bless His holy name! Bless the Lord, O my soul, and*
> *forget not all His benefits: Who forgives all your*

iniquities, Who heals all your diseases, Who redeems your life from destruction, Who crowns you with lovingkindness and tender mercies, Who satisfies your mouth with good things, so that your youth is renewed like the eagle's. (Psalm 103:1–5; emphasis added)

Now that sounds like some good benefits if only I could see them working in your life.

God's benefits for us are not spiritual. We are supposed to be manifesting His benefits to be a witness for Him on earth. The problem is that we can't manifest His benefits when we choose to live our lives according to the flesh and not according to the Spirit.

For though by this time you ought to be teachers, you need someone to teach you again the first principles of the oracles of God, and you have come to need milk and not solid food. For everyone who partakes only of milk is unskilled in the word of righteousness, for he is a babe. But solid food belongs to those who are of full age, that is, those who by reason of use have their senses exercised to discern both good and evil. (Hebrews 5:12–14)

God intends for His children to grow up to be what He's purposed them to be on earth.

Now I say that the heir, as long as he is a child, does not differ at all from a slave, though he is master of all, but is under guardians and stewards until the time appointed by the Father. (Galatians 4:1–2; emphasis added)

This text says that even though we are heirs, God is holding our inheritance back until we grow up and become the new man that He has called us to be on earth. Our lives are predestined. There's nothing you've been through or will ever go through that will catch God off guard. Our days and choices are not new to God. There's no sin that you can commit that the blood of Jesus has not paid for in full. There's no sin that you commit after salvation that His grace isn't sufficient to keep you standing firm in the family of God because where sin abounds, grace abounds much more! This is where Christians get stuck on the good news. We just want God to bless us on our terms; just wink at our foolishness as we live our lives any old kind of way.

When Paul was teaching this to the church in Rome and they heard the news about His grace, their response in Romans 6:1: *"What shall we say then? Shall we continue in sin that grace may abound?"* God forbids that response! Remember the woman caught in the act of adultery? Jesus asked her, "Where are those accusers of yours? Has no one condemned you?" When she saw none, He said, "Neither do I condemn you; go *and sin no more.*"

We grow in our obedience to the King. And when we disobey, His grace keeps us in the family of God, but there is no spiritual growth. You will have to take the same test over and over again until you pass it. God promises you trials and tribulations in your walk with Him. And while the enemy is bringing all he can to tempt you, God is allowing it as a test that your faith would be proven. We don't grow in the good times but when all hell is breaking loose in our lives. We have to stand in adversity and know that God wouldn't have allowed this to come upon us if He didn't equip us to be victorious in it.

God is the one who was bragging about Job to the enemy: "Have you considered My servant Job?" God foreknew what He equipped Job with, and we would've never seen it without the tribulation that he had to endure.

> *No temptation has overtaken you except such as is common to man; but God is faithful,* who will not allow *you to be tempted beyond what you are able, but with the temptation will also make the way of escape, that you may be able to bear it.*
> (1 Corinthians 10:13; emphasis added)

Your victory is already set. The fix is in; He always causes you to triumph.

> *Therefore, having been justified by faith,* "We have peace with God through our Lord Jesus Christ, through whom also we have access by faith into this grace in which we stand, and rejoice in hope of the glory of God. And not only that, but we also glory in tribulations, *knowing that tribulation produces perseverance; and perseverance, character; and character, hope.*" (Romans 5:1–4; emphasis added)

Our lives are predestined. That means that God has already made the way for you to become all that He has called you to become so that you would receive your inheritance on earth.

CHAPTER 2

Transformation

Religion versus Kingdom

RELIGION IS NOT the kingdom. Religion, or the fivefold ministry, is a product of the fall of man that is designed to reintroduce you to God and His ways and to teach you who you are in Him after being born again and how to relate to Him by faith. This is where we learn the fundamentals of God and begin our growth with our new spiritual man. You can have services every week and still not experience or even know anything about the kingdom of God, especially if it's not being taught. Man can only lead you where he's willing to go and can only teach you what he knows. Paul said, "Follow me as I follow the Lord." The Holy Spirit is present on earth today with a specific mandate from the King to lead His church into all truth. Man cannot lead you to the kingdom of God on his calling alone. If he or she does not have an understanding of the kingdom, how can they teach it?

I remember a particular service I was attending at my local church when I was in my early twenties. The pastor came in with this roll of paper, which looked like a scroll because it was all one piece. I'm not sure if he said someone asked him in the church if he would teach us about the kingdom of God or what actually caused him to do what he does. But what I remember from that service was he took that roll of paper, held one end, threw it to unroll from the pulpit all the way down the aisle, and said, "This is all the scriptures on the kingdom of God." And the church was amazed. But he didn't have a clue what to say about it or where to begin, so we went on with church as usual. This is not to say that if you have been attending a church and never heard the kingdom of God preached, your pastor is a bad person and God did not call them even that you should not be going there. It simply means that they probably were not taught about the kingdom of God themselves. You can spend four years or more in seminary and get your degree in Christian theology and come to find that it wasn't one class or one book on the kingdom of God and that is all Jesus preached. You can only teach what you know, but what you know is not all there is to know. There is only one who is omniscient—all-knowing—and that is the Holy Spirit. And He is here to guide us into all truth.

Our generation grew up in Catholicism, and in our seminary, we were taught the philosophies of men like St. Augustine and Martin Luther for example—men who lived and died in the 1500s. Again, not saying that these were bad men, but neither one of them had anything about the kingdom of God in their thesis, and somehow Christianity has relayed the foundational beliefs of men who based their theories on their own personal experiences and knowledge. The church of our Lord Jesus Christ started fifteen hundred years before these scholars that the church today hangs their entire belief system on.

In our homes we are to follow Proverbs 22:6: *"Train up a child in the way he should go: and when he is old, he will not depart from it."* Now I'm not saying every parent got this wrong, but I know this wasn't the norm in my community. There was nobody representing the kingdom of God in my neck of the woods—not in our homes, schools, jobs, marriages, friends, families, or even our churches. These are the very places God intends for us to be His witnesses. We witness with our lives, not just our mouths. That's why the Lord rebuked the religious leaders of that day.

*For I say to you, that unless your righteousness
exceeds the righteousness of the scribes and Pharisees,*

you will by no means *enter the kingdom of heaven.*
(Matthew 5:20; emphasis added)

The Pharisees talked a good religious talk, but their lives witnessed a lot of self-righteousness and condemnation toward other people. Now I do want to be clear that I am not bashing religion nor any of the scholars that have done the work that God has called them to do. But I am trying to make a distinction between religion and the kingdom of God. They are no way near the same.

Witnessing in the storm

Let's take the information thus far and see if we can see what the King is saying to His church. First is the word *church.* Its Greek word is *ekklisia,* which means temple, church, sanctuary, shrine, or tabernacle. The building where we go to worship and receive the Word of God is not the church, but it's the building where the church, which is the temple of God, gathers together to worship the King and receive His instructions or words of encouragement. So far, we see in His Word that God uses trials and tribulations to test us or cause what is now in us to grow up and become the new mature man that He's created us to be. And as you walk in obedience to the King, your life should be a witness to all men. We should be the light of the world, the salt of the earth, a peculiar people, a royal priesthood, a holy nation, living in this world but not like the world. There should be a distinction between the church and the world. We should know them by their fruits and their love for one another.

> *You, therefore, who teach another, do you not teach yourself? You who preach that a man should not steal, do you steal? You who say, "Do not commit adultery," do you commit adultery? You who abhor idols, do you rob temples? You who make your boast in the law, do you dishonor God through breaking the law? For "the name of God is blasphemed among the Gentiles because of you." (Romans 2:21–25)*

God is saying that the church has been misrepresenting His kingdom to the world, and His name is blasphemed among the Gentiles because of us. If I yoke myself to the world and its culture and I walk like they walk, talk like they talk, and feed my spirit the same things they feed on, then why should we think we will be able to provoke them to jealousy with our mouth alone? We would be no different from the Pharisees who were self-righteous and hypocritical in our witness. Jesus said, "If our righteousness does not exceed the righteousness of the scribes and Pharisees, we shall in no case enter into the kingdom of heaven." So when we go around telling people how they ought to live their lives, knowing we are living our lives according to the flesh and not according to the Spirit just like them and declaring to be righteous as you live your lives just like those you are trying to witness to is giving God a bad name on earth. This was the very reason Jesus rebuked the religious leaders of His day in His sermon given on the Mount of Olives known as the Olivet discourse.

When the trials of life come to test us, we need to know that God will not allow us to go through anything that we cannot bear. He does not just want us to go through it but to *grow* through it. We should not be moved by what we see or what they say, for we walk by faith and not by sight. So let's get fully dressed in the spirit and put the whole armor of God on. Keep your mind on Jesus, and He will give you perfect peace in the midst of your storm. Cast down every thought and imagination that would exalt itself over what God has already said, knowing that God is at work in you. Knowing that no weapon formed against you will be able to prosper. Knowing that what the enemy meant for your harm, God meant for your good. Knowing that all things work together for the good of those who love God and are called according to His purpose. I'm going through this right now, and I pray that God gets the glory in my stand for Him, for this too will pass.

The victory in every test belongs to the children of God because He always causes us to triumph. You may be going through something right now, and when you decide not to lean to your own understanding but just trust the Lord and the work that He is doing in you in this storm through this test that doesn't make any sense to you, knowing that He preplanned it for a purpose, you will come out of this and be better in some way because He is in it with you.

> *Therefore we do not lose heart. Even though our outward man is perishing, yet the inward man is being renewed day by day. For our light affliction, which is but for a moment, is working for us a far more exceeding and eternal weight of glory. While we do not look at the things which are seen, but at the things which are not seen. For the things which are seen are temporary, but the things which are not seen are eternal.* (2 Corinthians 4:16–18)

This storm will surely come to pass, and when it is over, I will be victorious and stronger in the Lord because of it. Therefore, I can praise Him in the midst of it: Have your way in me, my King!

The power to choose

God has given man his own will, which, in doing so, empowers him to choose against Him. When we choose against the Lord's commands, His laws, or His ways, it doesn't hurt God. Even if you intended to hurt Him in your rebellion, He's still good and He's still God. But *you* on the other hand? Disobeying God is not wise! God is for you, and His laws and commands are not given to you so you can't have any fun. They are given to you for your protection. When we choose to disobey God, He's not in heaven, saying, "Since they disobeyed Me, I'm going to get them." The consequences are built into the choices we make, whether obedience leads to life and righteousness or disobedience leads to death and destruction.

> *Do you not know that to whom you present yourselves slaves to obey, you are that one's slaves whom you obey, whether of sin leading to death, or of obedience leading to righteousness?* (Romans 6:16)

The devil has the church believing that it's okay to continue in your sins because God loves you and His grace is sufficient for you. Remember he is a master at deception. He even tried to temp the Word with the word. He just wants you to continue to be his slave. Notice in that verse that you are going to be a slave to one or the other, there is no middle ground. We either walk in obedience or disobedience. Salvation does not exempt the believer from obedience to the Lord, nor does it make the believer obey the Lord; the choice is man's alone.

> *The thief does not come except to steal, and to kill, and to destroy. I have come that they may have life, and that they may have it more abundantly.* (John 10:10)

God will respect your choice whether it's for Him or the enemy, but He wants you to understand that the choice you make determines your outcome.

> *See, I have set before you today life and good, death and evil, In that I command you today to love the Lord your God, to walk in His ways, and to keep His commandments, His statutes, and His judgments, that you may live and multiply; and the Lord your God will bless you in the land which you go to possess. But if your heart turns away so that you do not hear, and are* drawn away, *and worship other gods and serve them, I announce to you today that you shall surely perish; you shall not prolong your days in the land which you cross over the Jordan to go in and possess. I call heaven and earth as witnesses today against you, that I have set before you life and death, blessings and cursing;* therefore choose life, *that both you and your descendants may live.* (Deuteronomy 30:15–19)

The decision we have to make is either "yes, Lord" or "no, Lord." If "yes, Lord," then do what He commands. If "no, Lord," then do you, but you can't do both at the same time. We like to believe that if what we're doing is a good thing and not sinful, like fornication or murder, then God will understand because He knows our hearts and He knows we are good people. Well, in the great words of Dr. Phil, "How's that working for you?"

> *There is a way that seems right to a man, but its end is the way of death.* (Proverbs 14:12)

This is why it's so critical for those of us who have not lived or interacted with a kingdom to study kingdoms. Kingdoms are totally opposite from a democracy. There's no power to the people in a kingdom! In a kingdom, the majority rules nothing, and the king rules everything in his domain. When the king speaks, what he says becomes law. He doesn't have to run it through the senate or congress for approval, and he's not asking the people to vote and let him know how they feel about it. The king answers to nobody! He owns all the land in his domain and everything in it. His citizens sleep in houses that he provides and eat and drink his food. Nobody in a kingdom owns anything. The citizens' provisions and protection are provided by the king and he alone. They call it the commonwealth. There's no rich or poor or the haves and have-nots—that's capitalism. But the wealth is common. This is what you see in Acts chapter 5 with Ananias and Sapphira. In a kingdom, you own nothing. The king owns everything in his domain, including the people, the animals, the plants, the trees, the land, and the air that you breathe in the land. God is not a president, He's King!

> *The earth is the Lord's, and all its fullness, The world and those who dwell therein.* (Psalm 24:1)

We tolerate presidents, and we obey kings unless you find yourself guilty of treason or simply not in the king's favor or grace!

No middle ground

I remember when I was a child in grade school, we didn't have cell phones and social media to help us let a girl know we liked them or wanted them to be our girlfriend. So the hot thing going around for us, regular guys, was to write a little letter like "Do you like me?" or "Will you go out with me?" which meant "Will you be my girlfriend?" At the bottom of the note, you would write, "Circle yes or no," then you would give the letter to one of your boys to take it to her while you hide. Just leaving those two options sometimes puts too much pressure on a third grader, and she sends your note back with no circle on the yes or no but would write "maybe" and circle that.

Well, it seems that spirit has crept into the church today, and I'm about to expose it. God so loved the world that He gave His Son up for a ransom for many.

> *For* He made Him *who knew no sin to be sin for us, that we might become the righteousness of God in Him.* (2 Corinthians 5:21; emphasis added)

Jesus obeys the King all the way to the cross, demonstrating His love for us and the Father in His obedience to Him.

> *Therefore My Father loves Me, because I lay down My life that I may take it again. No one takes it from Me, but I lay it down of Myself. I have power to lay it down, and I have power to take it again. This command I have received from My Father.* (John 10:17–18)

The Son sends the Holy Spirit, also known as the comforter or the helper, full of grace and mercy to reveal the truth to us and the plan of God for our lives and to help us to transform into this new creation, to put it in a nutshell.

Therefore, if anyone is in Christ, he is a new creation; old things have passed away; behold, all things have become new. (2 Corinthians 5:17)

Now the spirit of God, speaking to us through Paul in Romans 12:1–2:

I BESEECH you therefore, brethren, by the mercies of God, that you present your bodies a living sacrifice, holy, acceptable to God, which is your reasonable service. And do not be conformed to this world, but be transformed by the renewing of your mind, that you may prove what is that good and acceptable and perfect will of God. (Emphasis added)

When the King commands you to do something, we can't circle "maybe" on the bottom of the note. God told King Saul in 1 Samuel 15 to go and attack Amalek and utterly destroy all that they had and not spare them but kill the men, women, children, babies, ox, sheep, camels, and donkeys. But King Saul, after killing all the people, decided to spare Agag and the best of the sheep, the oxen, the fatlings, the lambs, and all that was good and was unwilling to utterly destroy them. Everything despised and worthless was utterly destroyed. Then God rejected Saul as king. When Samuel checked Saul, he said he kept all the good stock so he could make sacrifices to God, but he did kill all those people for Him. I heard another quote and not sure from whom or if this is how it went. Obedience to God is either black or white; partial obedience is not a substitute for gray. If you heard that saying before, then you may know that I might have quoted it wrong, so I'll just close this chapter with Jesus's parable on the two sons when the chief priest and elders asked Him by what authority He did the things that He did.

But what do you think? A man had two sons, and he came to the first and said, "Son, go, work today in my vineyard." He answered and said, "I will not," but afterward he regretted it and went. Then he came to the second and said likewise. And he answered and said, "I go, sir," but he did not go. Which of the two did the will of his father? They said to Him, the first. Jesus said to them, "Assuredly, I say to you that tax collectors and harlots enter the kingdom of God before you." For John came to you in the way of righteousness, and you did not believe him; but tax collectors and harlots believed him; and when you saw it, you did not afterward relent and believe him. (Matthew 21:28–32; emphasis added)

The Bible teaches against *maybe* or gray. God doesn't want his children straddling the fence, one foot in the world and one in the church. He wants you to be clear!

But let your Yes be Yes, and your No, No. For whatever is more than these is from the evil one. (Matthew 5:37)

The King says, "Circle one or the other, maybe is not an option," lest He likens us to the church of the Laodiceans found in Revelation 3:15–16:

I know your works, that you are neither cold nor hot. I could wish you were cold or hot. So then, because you are lukewarm, and neither cold nor hot, I will vomit you out of My mouth.

Kingdom Requirements

Heavens Domain

FOR ME TO get this point across and for you to understand the things coming later in this book, I have to make sure we don't allow the phrase "the kingdom of God" to just be another religious phrase. The kingdom of God is a country! There are one hundred ninety-five countries in the world today. China is a country, India is a country, and the United States is a country, just to name a few. With that being said, to understand the ministry of Jesus, we have already seen thus far what He wasn't. The Pharisees and Sadducees thought the Messiah would be a religious man and come and settle their differences while the Sadducees didn't believe in the resurrection from the dead or the existence of spirits but held their faith in the written law alone. We also saw how Jesus was not moved by those zealots who tried to get Him to form a coup, overthrow the Roman Empire, and establish a natural kingdom on earth. That was Judas Iscariot's mindset.

Some believers today say things such as the temple being rebuilt in Jerusalem or Daniel missing the timing in his prophecy because they, too, are awaiting Jesus to return and establish a natural kingdom on earth. Jesus came to earth and submitted to His Father as an ambassador from the country of heaven, only to do the will of His

Father, the King who reigns in heaven. When an ambassador shows up, the whole country is present. If an ambassador from India came to the United States, when he walked in the room, India just came in the room. An ambassador never represents himself or gives you his personal opinion, he only speaks on behalf of his country. You ask him any question and his response will be, "My government's position on the matter is…" Therefore, he is there to represent the country and has been authorized to speak on the whole country's behalf. And if you offended an ambassador, you just offended the whole nation because you did not personally like the way he looked at you.

Jesus made statements like, "For I have not spoken of Myself, but the Father who sent Me, He gave Me a commandment, what I should say and what I should speak"—not only did Jesus represent His heavenly Father with what He said but in what He did as well. For He says, "Most assuredly, I say to you, the Son can do nothing of Himself, but what He sees the Father do; for whatever He does, the Son also does in like manner."

They asked Him, "Show us the Father."

He said, "When you see Me, you see the Father!"

One more thing I would like to point out before I get into my next topic: We see how Jesus was never persuaded by religious people or zealots who had their own philosophy on what the law and prophets taught, but He let their blindness remain and the gospel of the kingdom to remain a mystery to them, saying "Whoever has ears to hear, let them hear what the Spirit is saying to the church."

Let's look at this passage before we move on:

> *Therefore whoever confesses Me before men, him I will also confess before My Father* who is in heaven. *But whoever denies Me before men, him I will also deny before My Father* who is in heaven. Do not think *that I came to bring peace on earth. I did not come to bring peace* but a sword. *For I have come to set a man against his father, a daughter against her mother, a daughter-in-law against her mother-in-law; and a man's enemies will be those of his own*

> *household. He who loves his father or mother more than Me is not worthy of Me. And he who loves his son or daughter more than Me is not worthy of Me. And he who does not take his cross and follow after Me is not worthy of Me. He who finds his life will lose it, and he who loses his life for My sake will find it.* (Matthew 10:32–39; emphasis added)

Now I shared all of that to first see heaven or the kingdom of heaven as a country. And even though Jesus is King of kings and Lord of lords, at the time of His ministry on earth, He had not yet received His kingdom. That reality was the joy that was set before Him that enabled Him to endure the cross. In His earthly ministry, we should try to see Him as an ambassador because everywhere He went, He said the kingdom of God is here and He was commanded what to say and do and did. He never spoke of Himself. I know that the three wise men came to worship the King of the Jews or that Pilate straight asked Him, "Are you a king?" and Jesus said, "I am," and the inscription "Jesus the Nazarene, King of the Jews." But for the sake of His ministry on earth, I liken Him to an ambassador to help clarify His ministry like a parable. He's lion and lamb, king and servant, and much, much more! Let us also keep in mind that the world was made by the king in the unseen country, and the seen was created from the unseen.

Law and grace

Paul dealt with the subject of law and grace intensely in his writing to the church in Rome, and somehow, religion has magnified grace and nullified the law. We know there is no way we would be able to serve the Lord without grace because it was by His grace that we were saved—the free unmerited favor and mercy of God bestowed upon us as sinners because He so loved us, that if it had not been for the grace of God, we would still be dead in our sins and bound to eternal damnation. Thank God for grace!

But as Paul explains in his writings, grace is not a license to sin! God forbid! Grace is an extended opportunity to keep the law again; it covers you when you fall or make mistakes. It is God keeping you in right standings with Him. We see it with the woman who was caught in the very act of adultery. Jesus could have allowed her to be stoned to death because it was His law she had broken, but His grace was sufficient for her. And the Lord said to her, "Go and sin no more," or go and keep the law again.

When we live our lives as if we can continue in sin, which many Christians do because they know they can get forgiveness, God calls that iniquity. When we choose to live our lives as Christians in iniquity, we will not enter the kingdom of God. That type of choice causes you to live under another law, the law of sin and death; see Romans chapters 7 and 8, all of it. I know some say, "The law is under the old covenant, and we are in the new covenant." Jesus did not come to do away with the law but to fulfill it. Under the new covenant, because of what the Lord has done, there is no need for us to go to the high priest and have him offer up animal sacrifices on our behalf for our sins because Jesus, as the sacrificial lamb, fulfilled the law of Moses and ended the sacrifice of the Passover lamb with His blood, becoming the propitiation for our sins. Now our righteousness is not based upon our works anymore but upon our faith.

Now Jesus establishing a new covenant has nothing to do with the law. Every country has laws you have to abide by, and those laws build the culture of that country. Jesus came to earth all during His ministry and even forty days after His resurrection. He was teaching the people about the kingdom of God, which is a country in which all countries have their own laws, so why has the charismatic movement substituted God's laws for grace? You cannot have a country that operates on grace with no laws and expect order in that country! Can you imagine the United States of America with no laws but only grace and think that there will be order in that country? No, it would be chaos and mayhem if man was free to do as they please and their actions were covered by grace. You can kill, steal, and destroy all you want.

With no laws, that would produce a very unhealthy culture, to say the least. Paul says in Romans 7:16 that the law is good. Jesus says in Matthew 5:17, *Do not think that I came to destroy the Law or the Prophets. I did not come to destroy but to fulfill.* The birth of every country starts with laws that all who live there must abide by, and no one is to live above them. Those laws create the culture of that country. How would God have order in His kingdom and not chaos without laws and then tell us that He does everything decently and in order? When God brought the people of Israel out of Egypt and turned them from slaves into a nation, the first thing He gave them was the law—not power, not an anointing, but the law.

Let's look at the story of the rich young ruler:

> *Now behold, one came and said to Him, "Good Teacher, what good thing shall I do that I may have eternal life?" So He said to him, "Why do you call Me good? No one is good but One, that is, God. But if you want to enter into life,* keep the commandments. *" He said to Him, "Which ones?" Jesus said, "You shall not murder, you shall not commit adultery, you shall not steal, you shall not bear false witness, honor your father and your mother, and, you shall love your neighbor as yourself." The young man said to Him, "All these things I have kept from my youth. What do I still lack?" Jesus said to him, "If you want to be perfect, go, sell what you have and give to the poor, and you will have treasure in heaven; and come, follow Me." But when the young man heard that saying, he went away sorrowful, for he had great possessions. Then Jesus said to His disciples, "Assuredly, I say to you that it is hard for a rich man to enter the Kingdom of Heaven. And again I say to you, it is easier for a camel to go through the eye of a needle than for a rich man to enter the Kingdom of God."* (Mark 19:16–24; emphasis added)

First, I wanted you to see that he told him the way to enter into life was to keep the commandments. When he asked which ones, Jesus started running down the list of the same laws Moses received on Mount Sinai in the old covenant. But if he wanted to be perfect, Jesus told him to sell all he had and give to the poor. But because he had much, he wasn't feeling that. Why did Jesus tell the rich young ruler that? I know the United States struggles with this passage because growing up in a democracy, which functions by capitalism that teaches us to be independent, it says go for yours by any means necessary. Get all you can, put it in a can, and sit on the can. That's pretty much how that rich ruler probably accumulated his wealth.

You see, in a kingdom, the king owns everything. In Christianity, we think that if you pay your tithe, then the 90 percent is yours, which is not true; you own nothing in the kingdom. Your tithe is tax for your heavenly country so it can be meat in His house on His earthly domain also known as a colony. Independence is an enemy in a kingdom. In a kingdom culture, they have what they call a commonwealth. There are no poor people in a kingdom. All your needs are met by the king. You as a citizen are the king's responsibility. So I'm trusting that you will read Romans chapters 7 and 8 and see if Paul does away with the Law in any way.

Sacrifices of animals and things of that nature are what Christ fulfilled on the cross when the veil was torn in two. Therefore, we have to learn the laws of the kingdom of God and obey them like in any other country. Let's hear what the King says in Matthew 7:13–14:

> *Enter by the narrow gate; for wide is the gate and broad is the way that leads to destruction, and there are many who go in by it. Because narrow is the gate and difficult is the way which leads to life, and there are few who find it.*

You will understand later if you've not seen it so far; this is talking about the colony here on earth. A *colony* is a country or area under the full or partial political control of another country, typically a distant one, and occupied by settlers from that country.

Bearing fruit

There are over four thousand active religions in the world today, and Christianity is one. The four largest religious groups are Christianity, with 2.4 billion followers; followed by Islam, with 1.9 billion followers; then Hinduism, with 1.2 billion followers; and Buddhism, with a half billion followers. The fastest-growing religion in the twenty-first century is Islam. Despite what the media labels the conflict we have with other nations, these wars and attacks we see always have a religious dynamic to it. Destructive acts are carried out in the name of God. Even when you label your cause as radical Christians and go out blowing up abortion clinics, I promise you, the King of Glory is not in that! It's not in His nature!

The devil, on the other hand, has come to kill, steal, and destroy—who is a master deceiver that may come to you in sheep's clothing, the father of lies, roaming the land to see who he can use to do his bidding. And while he has the church divided, confused, and after their personal agendas pointing their fingers at everybody else except themselves, of course, the world is going to hell in a hand-basket, and the answer to all these problems lies within you. Greater is He that's within you than he that is in the world. We have exactly what this world is crying out for, housed within every believer. But we're too busy asking the King for Cadillacs, big houses, jobs, spouses, healings, and prosperity. To us, it's all about self-image. It's time for the church to let God arise and His enemies be scattered and to let the King of Glory come in. How do we do that?

> If *My people who are called by My name will* humble themselves, *and* pray *and* seek My face, *and* turn from *their wicked ways, then I will hear from heaven, and will forgive their sin and heal* their land. (2 Chronicles 7:14; emphasis added)

Trust me when I say that the enemy knows all about the kingdom of God, and if the church ever found out about it, there would be nothing he could do to stop the church from exposing and destroying all he's worked so hard to do. The gate of hell would not prevail against the church! I'm trusting that you read Romans 7 and 8 as I asked before getting here and see that there are two different laws at work in you every day—absolutely at war with each other in you, about you. This is why it is a must to take up your cross daily and crucify the flesh, freeing yourself from the law and enabling you to walk according to the things of the Spirit. There is no other way to even relate to your heavenly Father but by His Spirit.

> *God is a Spirit: and they that worship Him must worship Him in spirit and in truth.* (John 4:24)

The question that I'm hoping is rising in your spirit in all of this is, What are we going to do? Not God but *us*—the church! Will we rise up and be His disciples or sit back and call ourselves prayer warriors and do nothing because we already prayed about it? Let's hear the words of our King and see if we can hear what the Spirit is saying to the church.

> *Not everyone who says to Me, Lord, Lord, shall enter the kingdom of heaven, but he who does the will of My Father in heaven. Many will say to Me in that day, Lord Lord, have we not prophesied in Your name, cast out demons in Your name, and done many wonders in Your name? And then I will declare to them, I never knew you; depart from Me, you who practice lawlessness! Therefore whoever hears these sayings of Mines, and does them, I will liken him to a wise man who built his house on the rock. And the rain descended, the floods came, and the winds blew and beat on that house; and it did not fall, for it was founded on the rock. But everyone who hears these sayings of Mine, and does not do them, will be like a foolish man who built his house on the sand. And the rain descended, the floods came, and the winds blew and beat on that*

house; and it fell. And great was its fall. (Matthew 7:21–27)

Now if you're not convinced by now that the kingdom is here now and not in some distant future, then this passage should terrify you. But still, I'm hoping it gets your attention enough that we understand it's not the hearers that please God or positions in the fivefold ministry that exempt you from being able to enter in but the *doer* of His Father's will—that's the key to the door! Let's not be like the fig tree on the road when the Master Himself had a need, and it was no fruit. We ought to know His disciple when we see them by their fruits and their love for another. We will never be able to love the world out of darkness into His marvelous light in our flesh. But the spirit of God is still on earth, in the colony, as the helper, comforter, and governor, full of the love of God, ready to flow from our bellies like living waters. But our disobedience to the King dams it up.

Let's close this portion with Paul's letter to the church in Galatia.

> *I say then: Walk in the Spirit, and you shall not fulfill the lust of the flesh. For the flesh lusts against the Spirit, and the Spirit against the flesh; and these are contrary to one another, so that you do not do the things that you wish. But if you are led by the Spirit, you are not under the law. Now the works of the flesh are evident, which are: adultery, fornication, uncleanness, lewdness, idolatry, sorcery, hatred, contentions, jealousies, outbursts of wrath, selfish ambitions, dissensions, heresies, envy, murders, drunkenness, revelries, and the like; of which I tell you beforehand, just as I also told you in time past, that those who practice such things will not inherit the kingdom of God. But the fruit of the Spirit is love, joy, peace, longsuffering, kindness, goodness, faithfulness, gentleness, self-control. Against such there is no law. And those who are Christ's have crucified the flesh with its passions and desires. If we live in*

the Spirit, let us also walk in the Spirit. Let us not become conceited, provoking one another, envying one another. (Galatians 5:16–26; emphasis added)

Yes, Paul is teaching about the kingdom of God and wasn't even one of the twelve disciples; in fact, he was a notorious enemy of the church at that time.

Kingdom Applications

Kingdom Blessings

JESUS SPOKE TO the multitudes in parables to keep the mysteries of the kingdom of God hidden from those who were not seeking revelation. Revelational knowledge will cost you. We saw in that passage in 2 Chronicles that God was saying to seek His face, not His hands. I'm a father, and if my children only came to me when they wanted something and showed no interest in getting to know me as a person, then I, too, would feel a certain way about that. We need to understand that God is a good, loving father who's always for us and is always willing to answer our prayers. We assume that if He doesn't give us what we ask for or do what we ask of, He doesn't answer prayers. He answered, you just didn't like the answer. No is an answer, and for good reason.

For you with children, do you say yes to all your kid's requests? Let's remember the words of John F. Kennedy sometimes when we go to the Father in prayer and "ask not what your country can do for you, ask what you can do for your country." He was a president, and God is King! He wishes above all things that you would prosper and be in health even as your soul prospers. For it is your Father's good pleasure to give you the kingdom, which is your inheritance. We need to repent, which again means to change the way we think. God wants you to enjoy an abundant life here on earth. In fact, that's what He's trying to get you to grow into.

I hope you wouldn't give your child a Lamborghini and their own mansion at the age of four just because they asked you. God gets no glory out of His children's lives when they're broke, busted, and disgusted. Jesus didn't take those stripes on His back for kicks. But He was wounded for our transgressions, and He was bruised for our iniquities. And the chastisement of our peace was upon Him, and with His stripes, we are healed. He did that for us when we were still sinners. Now that we belong to the family of God, He wants to bless you so much that it will provoke the world to jealousy. That's how He intends to bless you. He wants to give you houses that you won't have to build and vineyards you wouldn't have to plant, without you even having to ask!

> *Therefore I say to you, don't worry about your life, what you will eat or what you will drink; nor about your body, what you will put on. Is not life more than food and the body more than clothing? But seek first the kingdom of God and His righteousness, and all these things shall be added to you. (Matthew 6:25, 33)*

> *No one can serve two masters; for either he will hate the one and love the other, or else he will be loyal to the one and despise the other. You cannot serve God and money. (Matthew 6:24)*

Even though we are in this world, we are not to be influenced by it or become one with it and its systems. Here on earth, money is the substance of things we hoped for, the evidence of things seen. But we, on the other hand, walk by faith and not by sight! The currency of the kingdom of God is faith! Now faith is the substance of things we hoped for, the evidence of things not seen. And without faith, it is impossible to please Him, for he who comes to God must believe that He is and that He is a rewarder of *those who diligently seek Him.*

Now for you all who know your Bibles, know that all the things I just shared are in Scripture, and I usually would have put those scriptures in the writings, but I started chasing rabbits and got off track. So hopefully, that was for somebody, and you might have to look at it as a parable and seek the scriptures yourself on these. The good news is, I have bound the spirit of Elmer Fudd off me, and no more rabbit season. Back to the parables.

Parable of the Soils

For now, there are two parables I want to look at. In these two parables, Jesus plainly explains them to His disciples so we cannot mess up the interpretations of them. They are both found in Matthew chapter 13. But before we look at them, there are some tools I want you to have that will better help you see or understand as we dive in. There's a pattern in the Bible all throughout it such as first comes the natural, then the spiritual. This is where you get the terms, types, and shadows. First, we see the shadow, then the reality. For example, God makes a promise to Abraham that He would make him a great nation and his descendants as numerous as the stars in the sky while his wife was barren and he was up in age. Well, as time passed by, Abraham and Sarah didn't see God fulfilling the promise when they thought and how they thought He should, so they decided to help God out and produced Ishmael (natural/shadow). Later, God gave them Isaac (spiritual/promise). Again, with Isaac's twins, first-born Esau—whom I hated (natural) but secondborn Jacob—whom I loved (promise/spiritual). Or Adam (type and shadow) and second Adam (Christ/reality). Moses and the Son of Man (prophet like Moses/reality)—too many to list but hopefully you get the picture. Remember Romans 15:4, *"For whatever things were written before were written for our learning, that we through the patience and comfort of the Scriptures might have hope."* The Old Testament scriptures are all they had when Paul wrote this letter to the church in Rome. There was no New Testament Scripture yet.

Therefore, to help you interpret your Bible correctly, the New Testament is in the Old Testament concealed, and the Old Testament is in the New Testament revealed. Or the New Testament is in the Old Testament contained, and the Old Testament is in the New Testament explained. In other words, Old Testament folks looked forward to the promises—the shadow—but we New Testament folks got the reality! John 5:39 says, "You search the Scriptures, for in them you think you have eternal life; and these are they which testify of Me." Jesus just said that the Old Testament scriptures testify of Him, which is all the early church had to go by as they lived in the birthing years of the church of Jesus Christ and wrote the very letters that would become our New Testament references, which was not their intent. They just didn't have televisions and cell phones and all our modern-day ways to communicate with each other, and the letter was the best way to speak to the masses.

Now, let's look at Matthew 13:3–9:

> *Then He spoke many things to them in parables, saying: Behold, a sower went out to sow. And as he sowed, some seed fell by the wayside; and the birds came and devoured them. Some fell on stony places, where they did not have much earth; and they immediately sprang up because they had no depth of earth. But when the sun was up they were scorched, and because they had no root they withered away. And some fell among thorns, and the thorns sprang up and choked them. But others fell on good ground and yielded a crop: some a hundredfold, some sixty, some thirty. He who has ears to hear, let him hear!*

Jesus spoke this parable to the multitude, and we will see what was in the mind of Jesus when He said these words to the crowd. I first would like to remind you of Hebrews 13:8, *"Jesus Christ is the same yesterday, today, and forever."* Now let's picture ourselves as part of the crowd and listen to these words. If these words were all we heard, then it could be possible for us to hear the story of the sower who went out to sow, threw his seed everywhere, and produced very little crops because of his sporadic spread of seeds. This is how many

Christians live—by their own interpretation. Jesus still operates the same today as He did yesterday and will be tomorrow.

When we look at what Jesus meant, I want you to understand He's only revealing the meaning to His disciples. No one in the crowd is in on the true nature of His words. But I promise you because they heard from God, they're telling their friends what says the Lord from their own private interpretation. He reveals to the obedient, cross-bearing, diligent-seeking disciples. Let's see what they got out of it. After explaining to His disciples why He speaks to the crowd in parables, He says to them (Matthew 13:18–23; emphasis added),

> *Therefore hear the parable of the sower: When anyone hears the word of the kingdom, and does not understand it, then the wicked one comes and snatches away what was sown in his heart. This is he who received seed by the wayside. But he who received the seed on stony places, this is he who hears the word and immediately receives it with joy; yet he has no root in himself, but endures only for a while. For when tribulation or persecution arises because of the word, immediately he stumbles. Now he who received seed among the thorns is he who hears the word, and the cares of this world and the deceitfulness of riches choke the word, and he becomes unfruitful. But he who received seed on the good ground is he who hears the word and understands it, who indeed bears fruit and produces: some a hundredfold, some sixty, some thirty.*

That's the verse we like to get our shout on, but I don't think the disciples were shouting even though they just received divine revelation from Emmanuel Himself. Jesus just explained to them what He saw when He was looking at the crowd. The crowd remains the same today. And if you don't see a thirty, sixty, and hundredfold return operating in your life personally, then you must examine the condition of your heart—which, in the parable, was the different types of ground the sower was sowing his seed—with the other three examples and get your soil prepared to produce and bear fruit because it would have to be one of the others.

Parable of the Wheat and Tares

Now just in case you didn't open your Bible to chapter 13 to look at these parables for yourself, I just want to make a reference about the disciples' question in verse 10: Why do you speak to them in parables? Jesus answers that question in verses 11–17. A parable is designed to allow the hearer to hear the truth and leave with no understanding of what they heard. Notice when the disciples got along with Jesus, they would ask for revelation and Jesus would begin to reveal it to them clearly because the parables would go over their heads too. This parable we are about to look at is about to shift me in a direction that I'm sure we'll be dealing with in the next chapter. If we were at church, I would say, "Turn to your neighbor and say, 'Let's go there.'"

> *Another parable He put forth to them saying: "The kingdom of heaven is like a man who sowed good seed in his field; but while men slept, his enemy came and sowed tares among the wheat and went his way. But when the grain had sprouted and produced a crop, then the tares also appeared. So the servants of the owner came and said to him, 'Sir, did you not sow good seed in your field? How then does it have tares?' He said to them, 'An enemy has done this.' The servants said to him, 'Do you want us then to go and gather them up?' But he said, 'No, lest while you gather up the tares you also uproot the wheat with them. Let both grow together until the harvest, and at the time of harvest I will say to the reapers, "First gather together the tares and bind them in bundles to burn them, but gather the wheat into my barns."'" (Matthew 13:24–30)*

This time, we won't give our own private interpretation because we understand—we weren't supposed to understand. But I do want to remind you that the Bible is full of types, shadows, and metaphors. For example, Jesus first came up to Peter when he had just come in from fishing and said, "Follow me and I will make you fishers of men." Now if Peter would've cast his net at men or got his fishing rod and placed a hook in your hamburger, well, it's safe to say he would probably have a fight on his hands, to say the least. Or remember when Jesus tells them, "Destroy this temple and in three days I will raise it back up." Their response is funny to us because we can read what he really meant. Or that famous phrase that reads, "You must be born again."

Nicodemus was a Pharisee, a ruler of the Jews, and a teacher of the law, but he couldn't pick up his Bible and read the New Testament like we can because it had not been written yet. So his response was, "How can a man be born when he is old? Can he enter a second time into his mother's womb and be born?" I know the mothers are glad that the Lord did not say yes! That phrase is not getting that type of response in the twenty-first century.

Now let's let Jesus interpret this parable and see where we end up at the end of this book.

> *Then Jesus sent the multitude away and went into the house. And His disciples came to Him, saying, "Explain to us the parable of the tares of the field." He answered and said to them: "He who sows the good seed is the Son of Man." The field is the world, the good seeds are the sons of the kingdom, but the tares are the sons of the wicked one. The enemy who sowed them is the devil, the harvest is the end of the age, and the reapers are the angels. Therefore as the tares are gathered and burned in the fire, so it will be at the end of this age. The Son of Man will send out His angels, and they will gather out of His kingdom all things that offend, and those who practice lawlessness, and will cast them into the furnace*

of fire. There will be wailing and gnashing of teeth. Then the righteous will shine forth as the sun in the kingdom of their Father. He who has ears to hear, let him hear! (Matthew 13:36–43; emphasis added)

First, I would like to point out that in the Old King James version, they used the word *world* in verses 30 and 40 but later corrected it in the New King James version. This makes a big difference in the meaning of what Jesus is saying. And second, Jesus is speaking plainly to His disciples in the house, answering their questions plainly at this particular time. He's not using parables or metaphors. As we move on, I want you to keep in mind here that in verse 39, He says, "The harvest is the end of the age," and in verse 40, He says, "So it will be at the end of *this age*." You're going to need that for the next chapter if you plan on continuing to read this book. It's about to get bumpy for a while and even controversial because of the way we have been taught in the past centuries. But I know the Lord will carry us through because of what He has for us on the other side of it.

Kingdom Conflicts

Pronouncing Judgments

I ASKED YOU to remember the words of Jesus as He was explaining to His disciples the meaning of the parable of the wheat and the tares when He said, "So will it be at the end of *this age*." After correcting the translation from the original Greek to the English language, from world to age, we need to know what He means by *age*. When Jesus concluded His explanation to His disciples, you see in verse 41 the Son of Man sending His angels to gather out of His kingdom all things that offend and those who practice lawlessness. This is the Lord letting His disciples know that the resistance or persecution that the early church had to endure had a clock on it, *timing*. In verse 42, you see the tares cast into the furnace of fire. This is the *judgment* of the Lord. In verse 43, you see the righteous able to go forth with no more resistance just like the children of Israel when the pharaoh and his armies were drowned in the Red Sea. Moses said, "The enemies you see today you will see no more!" So we see in the conclusion that something is coming to an end and something can continue.

Now I would like to point out that when we see in the scripture the writer referring to a generation, a generation is sometimes used to speak of a period of forty years. Moses was on the backside of the desert for a generation. The people of Israel wandered in the wilderness for a generation. I said all that to speak of the generation that Jesus had begun in His earthly ministry in Matthew 4:17. Repent, for the kingdom of heaven is at hand; or change the way you think, for the kingdom of heaven has arrived. We know that Jesus was of the age of thirty when He began His earthly ministry, which would put His entire ministry between AD 30–34. We should also recall that God didn't take His people out of Egypt and straight into the land He promised them but into the wilderness for forty years to repent and get their minds renewed.

Now I would like to point out to you a very unique generation, the generation from AD 30–70. This generation is the only generation in the history of mankind called the transitional generation. The reason for that is, it's the only generation where the old covenant and the new covenant overlapped with one another. Jesus began His ministry under the old covenant of course and began to birth the new covenant. Therefore, *the age* that the Son of Man (which is Jesus, but in this parable, He uses the Son of Man analogy that is likened unto a prophet like Moses) is referring to is the old covenant or the Jewish mission coming to an end and the new covenant or the Gentile mission going forth without restriction. Jesus was basically pronouncing judgment on apostate Israel.

The New Testament is full of these references, and we're going to look at some of them. But first, I want you to understand the actual destruction of Jerusalem that took place in our history in AD 70. They surrounded the city, starved the people, and went in and demolished, massacred, and obliterated the Jews, busting into their houses and killing every Jew in sight. Millions of Jews were left dead in the streets, and the streets were filled with blood; and to top it off, they set the city on fire. Now that is actual facts of history, which we'll get more into later.

I want you to understand that what we know as the New Testament of scripture was all written in this transitional generation, including the book of Revelation that was written by John, the disciple whom Jesus loved. John died in AD 99 at the age of eighty-eight and was born in AD 11, the only disciple who lived past that destruction. The rest were killed for His name's sake as the servants of the Lord in that transitional generation. Remember when Jesus was telling Peter the death he would die for His name's sake, and Peter's response was, "What about John over here?" And Jesus says to him, "What is it to you that if I have him to remain till I come?" In other words, you do you Peter, and don't worry about what I have in store for John!

Some scholars say that John wrote the book of Revelation around AD 95–96 while other scholars date the writings of the book around AD 66–68. I'm definitely with the latter. As I already stated, all the writings of the New Testament were written in this transitional generation, pre-AD 70. I would encourage you to go back and look at how the book of Revelation even starts and ends. John is warning the church about something that he was shown that was about to take place in chapter 1:1–3, *"Behold, He is coming with clouds, and every eye will see Him, even they who pierced Him. And all the tribes of the earth will mourn because of Him. Even so, Amen."* I'm having to refrain from diving into the book of Revelation, that would be a book in itself. So let me have you also call into mind that the earth was only populated over there in the eastern part of the world. So we must take away all of what we are accustomed to—no cars, no trains, no planes, no buses, cell phones, computers, lights, etc. You get the picture, now let's go there.

Olivet Discourse

We know that it was the religious leaders of that day that had Jesus killed or crucified—the scribes, Pharisees, and Sadducees, along with those zealots who tried to get Him to lead them in a rebellion against Rome and establish His kingdom on earth. They were the main opposition that He had to face during His earthly ministry—not just them being successful in having Him crucified but at every turn all throughout His ministry. They were constantly plotting ways to kill Him or to trip Him up in the things that He said that they might accuse Him of some sort of blasphemy. These were the people Jesus had in mind when He made that famous quote in Matthew 11:12–13.

> *And from the days of John the Baptist until now, the kingdom of heaven suffers violence, and the violent take it by force. For all the prophets and the law prophesied until John.*

This is the motivation behind Jesus's Olivet discourse message, not only for the resistance He or the kingdom faced from them but for all the bloodshed of the prophets and righteous men that came before Him. Jesus is pronouncing His judgment for all that they were doing and the works of their forefathers. They had a self-righteous attitude toward the people and felt they should be put on a pedestal, exalting themselves. In Matthew 23, Jesus is *a judge* in the court of law, presenting the facts in the case against them in the kingdom of heaven. I encourage you to read the whole chapter and you'll see as He confronts His opposition publicly. He wasn't trying to sugarcoat it or say it in a nice way to be sure not to hurt anyone's feelings. In fact, with much name-calling and many woes, that is to say, I feel sorrow for you or I'm glad I'm not you in this case, expressing sorrow or despair, misfortune or trouble.

Let's look at a few verses to grasp the context of chapter 23, first starting with verses 1–3.

> *Then Jesus spoke to the multitudes and to His disciples, saying: "The scribes and the Pharisees sit in Moses' seat. Therefore whatever they tell you to observe, that observe and do, but do not do according to their works; for they say, and do not do."*

Now skipping down to verses 13–15 (emphasis added),

> *But woe to you, scribes and Pharisees, hypocrites! For you shut up the kingdom of heaven against men; for you neither go in yourselves, nor do you allow those who are entering to go in. Woe to you, scribes and Pharisees, hypocrites! For you devour widows' houses and for a pretense make long prayers.*

Therefore, you will receive greater condemnation. Woe to you, scribes and Pharisees, hypocrites! For you travel land and sea to win one proselyte, and when he is won, you make him twice as much a son of hell as yourselves.

This chapter is full of woes and name-calling, such as hypocrites, to give an idea of how the Lord was fed up with their pious, self-righteous attitudes. God would watch them go over to widows' houses and give them their long and elegant prayers, leaving them with the impression that all is well because they have prayed their special prayers over them but still leaving them in the same state they were in when they got there—hurting and confused, not knowing how they will make ends meet for themselves.

Now let's skip down to the last ten verses and first take a look at verses 29–36 (emphasis added).

Woe to you, scribes and Pharisees, hypocrites! Because you build the tombs of the prophets and adorn the monuments of the righteous, and say, "If we had lived in the days of our fathers, we would not have been partakers with them in the blood of the prophets." Therefore you are witnesses against yourselves that you are sons of those who murdered the prophets. Fill up then, the measure of your father's guilt. Serpents, brood of vipers! How can you escape the condemnation of hell? Therefore, indeed, I send you prophets, wise men, and scribes: some of them you will kill and crucify, and some of them you will scourge in your synagogues and persecute from city to city, that on you may come all *the righteous blood shed on the earth, from the blood of righteous Able to the blood of Zechariah, son of Berechiah, whom you murdered between the temple and the alter. Assuredly, I say to you,* all these things will come upon this generation.

Jesus has just slammed the gavel down with His judgment on apostate Israel and filled the measure of their guilt with their forefathers' sins and also the blood that would be shed by His death and His disciples whom He knew would also be their victims. In verse 36, He says that this judgment would be carried out on that generation. We see in our history this sentence was carried out in the destruction of Jerusalem in AD 70.

Now let's close with these last three verses, very familiar passages, verses 37–39 (emphasis added),

> *O Jerusalem, Jerusalem, the one who kills the prophets and stones those who are sent to her! How often I wanted to gather your children together, as a hen gathers her chicks under her wings,* but you were not willing! *See! Your house is left to you desolate; for I say to you, you shall see me no more till you say, Blessed is He who comes in the name of the Lord!*

Jesus publicly pronounces His judgment, or like He says, on the one who kills the prophets and stones those who are sent to her! These self-righteous, self-centered people were caught up in their traditions and rituals but neglected the weightier matters of the law—justice, mercy, and faith—found in verse 23, in a portion I skipped.

Matthew 24

Before we look at this very familiar and what seems to have become a very controversial passage of scripture, let's remember the parable of the wheat and the tares, the transitional generation, how long a generation is, and how Jesus always answers His disciples plainly—not in metaphors, types, and shadows because He was the reality of what they spoke of. He was revealing to His disciples the secrets and mysteries that had been hidden from the foundation of the world. He spoke one way to the multitudes but to His disciples. He spoke plainly with no secrets. Even the Father revealed to Peter who Jesus was.

Before we look at this passage, if you've been taught to interpret the scriptures by watching the news or reading your local newspaper to look at current events to understand what He is saying to His disciples, then how do we think the disciples would have understood Jesus as He answered them plainly if the revelation was hidden in events two thousand years later, which Jesus never plainly said? That's not how it works. Let scripture interpret scripture for it will not contradict itself. I promised you a bumpy ride for a few, so shift your spiritual ears in a four-wheel drive, and let's get through this together. Let's look at Matthew 24:1–35, and let's look at a statement Jesus makes in verse 34 first, then understand all the things He says before that verse is to be a part of His answer as we go back to verse one. That statement is, *"This generation will by no means pass away till all these things take place."*

Now let's go back and see what things He is referring to in this passage. Remember, Jesus had just finished dropping the gavel in His judgment on Jerusalem publicly in the temple, and His disciples were there. Matthew 24:1–35, starting with verses 1–2, states, "Then Jesus went out and departed from the temple, and His disciples came up to show Him the buildings of the temple. And Jesus said to them, 'Do you not see all these things? Assuredly, I say to you, not one stone shall be left here upon another, that shall not be thrown down.'" The disciples were trying to show Jesus the beauty and craftsmanship of the temple, and Jesus responded, "Did you all just hear the words that just came out of my mouth? Not one stone here shall be left upon another when my judgment is executed."

It just so happens that that very temple was destroyed in the destruction of Jerusalem, and not one stone was left upon another because, in the building of the temple, Israel used gold for mortar. And after the Roman's victory, they took the gold that was used for mortar from between the bricks, brick by brick. Now the disciples asked Jesus two questions: *"Now as He sat on the Mount of Olives, the disciples came to Him privately, saying, Tell us, when will these things be? And what will be the sign of Your coming, and of the end of the age?"* (Matthew 24:3; Greek word *aionos*, which refers to an age).

Now Jesus is about to answer their questions, and I want you to notice that nowhere in His answer did He tell them, "Don't worry about it, you won't see these signs for thousands of years so you will be long gone." But we will see Him keep referring to them personally and telling them that they would be killed, all of them, except for John. Verse 4 says, *"And Jesus answered and said to them; 'Take heed that no one deceives you.'"*

When studying the Bible, they teach you to exegete the text—it's the process of discovering the original intended meaning of a passage of Scripture. In other words, it can't mean to you what it didn't mean to them first. We see in verse 4 that Jesus said to them and told them to let no one deceive them. I was going to skip some as I did in the previous chapter but decided it's a must to look at it all. I will stop briefly in verse 15, but the rest, I think, is clear enough. Verses 5–15 state,

> *For many will come in My name, saying I am the Christ, and will deceive many. And* you *will hear of wars and rumors of wars. See that* you *are not troubled; for all these things must come to pass, but the end is not yet. For nation will rise against nation, and kingdom against kingdom. And there will be famines, pestilences, and earthquakes in various places. All these are the beginning of sorrows. Then they will deliver* you *up to tribulation and* kill you, *and* you *will be hated by all nations for My name's sake. And then many will be offended, will betray one another, and will hate one another. Then many false prophets will rise up and deceive many. And because lawlessness will abound, the love of many will grow cold. But he who endures to the end shall be saved. And this* gospel of the kingdom *will be preached in all the world as a witness to all the nations, and then the end will come. Therefore, when* you *see the abomination of desolation, spoken of by Daniel the prophet, standing in*

the holy place [whoever reads, let him understand].
(Emphasis added)

Notice: The warning in parenthesis written by Matthew sounds just like the warnings we look at in Revelation. This generation could not afford to get it wrong. Their very lives depended on understanding what the Lord was saying to them. The abomination of desolation spoken of by Daniel is found in Daniel 12:11, and he puts a clock on it, and there's no way he's saying over two thousand years. But Luke, in his recordings of this passage, explains what the abomination of desolation is more clearly. Luke 21:20 says, *"But when you see Jerusalem surrounded by armies, then know that its desolation is near."* Matthew puts in parenthesis for the reader of that letter, not thinking it was New Testament scripture but just the letter he intended to be for the ministry they were called to for that generation. "Whoever reads this letter, let him understand." We know the disciples understood as you see how it was worded in Luke's account.

> *Then let those who are in Judea flee to the mountains. Let him who is on the housetop not go down to take anything out of his house. And let him who is in the field not go back to get his clothes.*

Josephus was a Roman and military leader, who also was a Jewish historian best known for writing the Jewish wars. He says in his writings that when the Romans began their siege and started setting up to surround Jerusalem, the Christians fled the city to the mountains. The Romans surrounded them to cut off their food supply, and after starving the people, they came in and wiped them out.

> *But woe to those who are pregnant and to those who are nursing babies in those days! And pray that your flight may not be in winter or on the Sabbath. For then there will be great tribulation, such as has not been since the beginning of the world until this time, no, nor ever shall be. And unless those days*

were shortened, no flesh would be saved; but for the elect's sake *those days will be shortened.*

This started in March AD 70 and ended in September AD 70.

Then if anyone say to you, *look, here is the Christ! Or there! Do not believe it. For false Christ and false prophets will rise and show great signs and wonders to deceive, if possible, even the elect. See, I have told* you *beforehand. Therefore, if they say to you, look, He is in the desert! Do not go out; or look, He is in the inner rooms! Do not believe it. For as the lightning comes from the east and flashes to the west, so also will the coming of the Son of Man be. For wherever the carcass is, there the eagles will be gathered together. Immediately after the tribulation of those days the sun will be darkened, and the moon will not give its light; the stars will fall from heaven, and the powers of the heavens will be shaken.*

This verse is referring to apostate Israel. The sun is Israel, the moon is Jerusalem, and the stars are the rulers. Again, Jesus is not speaking over their heads but answering their questions; the disciples understood this language.

Then the sign of the Son of Man will appear in heaven, and then all the tribes of the earth will mourn, and they will see the Son of Man coming on the clouds of heaven with power and great glory.

Remember this statement when we looked at Revelation 1:7, and it also said that even those who pierced Him would see Him coming in the clouds. "Coming in the clouds" is a term used in the Old Testament describing God riding in on a cloud as His chariot to bring judgment upon a nation or people. See Isaiah 19:1 for an example.

> *And He will send His angels with a great sound of a trumpet, and they will gather together His elect from the four winds, from one end of heaven to the other.*

Remember the wheat and tares, the angels gathered the tares and destroyed them and then gathered the wheat.

> *Now learn this parable from the fig tree: When its branch has already become tender and puts forth leaves, you know that summer is near. So* you *also, when* you *see* all these things, *know that it is near—at the door!* Assuredly, *I say* to you, this generation *will by no means pass away till* all these things take place. *Heaven and earth will pass away, but My words will by no means pass away.*

I want to give you a verse that also shows you Jesus is speaking to that generation in Matthew 16:28 (emphasis added).

> *Assuredly, I say to you,* there are some standing here who shall not taste death *till they see the Son of Man coming in His kingdom.*

Now if it were some folk living in this world that was over two thousand years old, I'm sure we would have heard about it by now.

CHAPTER 6

Kingdom Etiquette

Good and Judgment

THE CHURCH HAS made a habit of preaching and teaching one half of Jesus, the good and loving half. The half that reinsures us that He will never leave us nor forsake us and nothing can separate us from His love. His mercy endures forever, and of course, He died for our sins, etc. All are true and much more to His good side than that, but I'm going to put the grace of God back on His good side and tell you about the other side. Let's not forget what we just read about apostate Israel—His judgment!

He has the authority to baptize you with the Holy Ghost and fire. Judgment!

> *For the Father judges no one, but has committed all judgment to the Son, that all should honor the Son just as they honor the Father. He who does not honor the Son does not honor the Father who sent Him. Most assuredly, I say to you, he who hears My word and believes in Him who sent Me has everlasting life, and shall not come into judgment, but has passed from death into life. (John 5:22–24)*

The Bible tells us that the fear of the Lord is the beginning of wisdom, but there is no fear of the Lord when we make Him like Santa Claus. The church today is guilty of grace abuse, which is abnormal use. We understand drug abuse—how doctors go to school for eight years to learn about a substance like coca—sometimes used medically as a local anesthetic. If you've ever had any type of surgery where it was used, you would know it was a very good thing in its proper use. But Tyrone, on the other hand, dropped out of school in the seventh grade and finished his education in the hood and was taught how to take the coca plant and turn it into cocaine and make his money at the expense of his loved ones. That's drug abuse or abnormal use.

In other words, that is not what it was intended for. Grace is not a license to sin. Grace is given to us to cover us when we make mistakes. That's what the law could not do. That's what it means when it says the law kills. You can be a good moral law–abiding citizen; and the moment you break the law in any way, in your country and God's country, you will be found guilty and suffer the penalty according to the law. For no one is above the law (in theory). But if we follow after the Spirit, we're no longer under law but under grace. Therefore, the penalties for breaking the law do not affect your citizenship in the kingdom of heaven. You still have all your rights and all your benefits because you are covered by the grace of God! So what then? Do I *continue* in sin so grace may abound? *God Forbid!* He forbids you to continue in sin, but He has covered you by grace, and He expects you to get up when you fall and go and sin no more.

Proverbs 24:16 says, *"For a righteous man may fall seven times and rise again, but the wicked shall fall by calamity."* When the righteous fall or make mistakes, we can come boldly to the throne of grace, obtain mercy in our times of need, and keep on pressing toward the mark, all because of what Jesus has done for us. Second Corinthians 5:21 states, *"For He [the Father] made Him [the Son] who knew no sin to be sin for us, that we might become the righteousness of God in Him."* So grace definitely belongs on the good news side.

Now let's look at the other side. This is not to say it's a bad side because there is nothing bad in Him, but we must understand Him in His fullness. God intends for you to choose to live on His good side where all His promises to you can fully be enjoyed, but He is a just God, and He is no respecter of person. He watches over His word to perform it, and His word is a two-edged sword. If you obey His word, you will experience the good side where joy, peace, love, and righteousness—which is being in right standing with God—abide. But if you choose to disobey, not make a mistake but choose to go against His word, that's iniquity and that choice has the consequences built-in—frustration, depression, disappointment, sickness, heartache and pain, etc.

It's not that He's doing it to you but you bring it upon yourself because of your choices. Hebrews 4:12 says, *"For the word of God is living and powerful, and sharper than any two-edged sword, piercing even to the division of soul and spirit, and of joints and marrow, and is a discerner of the thoughts and intents of the heart."* God has given every man the power to choose. And when I say man, I mean mankind. Man comes in two models, male and female, and He has removed every barrier that would prevent you from succeeding. God knows what He has done for His children, and He knows there is nothing that can stop them.

Hosea 4:6 states, *"My people are destroyed for lack of knowledge. Because you have rejected knowledge, I also will reject you from being priest for Me; Because you have forgotten the law of your God, I also will forget your children."* He has always persuaded us to choose the right way: "Today I lay before you life and death, choose life"; "Adam, you can eat from any tree in the garden and it's all yours to enjoy except this one, the tree of good and evil." The tree of life was in the garden, but He gave man the power to choose.

Genesis 2:9 states, *"And out of the ground, the Lord God made every tree grow that is pleasant to the sight and good for food. The tree of life was also in the midst of the garden, and the tree of the knowledge of good and evil."* Adam could've eaten from the tree of life if he wanted, and all would've been well.

> *And the Lord God commanded the man, saying,*
> *"Of every tree of the garden you may freely eat; but*

*of the tree of the knowledge of good and evil you
shall not eat, for in the day that you eat of it you
shall surely die."* (Genesis 2:16–17)

God didn't create man to be a robot to carry out His will but
made him in His own image and likeness. If God didn't give man
the ability to choose, then he wouldn't be like God because God has
the power to make choices. Man was already like God, and the devil
deceived the woman by saying that God didn't want them to eat from
the tree of good and evil so they wouldn't be like what they already
were like, God. God intended to have an intimate relationship with
man as He ruled the seen from the unseen and that their relationship
be founded upon love. Just walking around with you in the cool of
the day type of relationship, and for Tyrone, just kickin' it wit-cha!

Malfunctioning saints

Now we can no longer play the blame game and ask Adam. "It
was that woman that You gave me." Adam blamed the woman and
God in one sentence for his choice to disobey God's command. It
didn't work for Adam, and even though it's still very popular today,
it still doesn't work for us.

> *Then God said, "Let Us make man in Our image,
> according to Our likeness; let them have dominion
> over the fish of the sea, over the birds of the air,
> and over the cattle, over all the earth and over every
> creeping thing that creeps on the earth."* (Genesis
> 1:26)

What did God mean in *our mage*? He means morale, spiritual
nature, and characteristics of a thing. And *our likeness*? It doesn't
mean to look like God but to function like He functions. How does
God function? He works by faith, and faith works by love, and He
creates by speaking and believing. Ruler—He rules in the heavens
that is His domain as King. He gives man the earth to have dominion

or rulership as king. He's King of kings and Lord of lords. God's plan was for Him to rule in the unseen world and for His children to rule in the seen. But Adam definitely threw a monkey wrench in the plan of God by choosing to rebel against the Lord's command. In that choice, man declared independence from the kingdom of heaven and the spirit of God left the world to man, for a season. I said for a season because God already had a plan to restore the kingdom of heaven back to His children.

God was not caught off guard, that's impossible! What I mean is a season to God. Second Peter 3:8 says, *"But, beloved, do not forget this one thing, that with the Lord one day is as a thousand years, and a thousand years as one day."* God does not live in time, He lives in eternity. He created time for man to live in. God does not have a birthday because God does not have a beginning; He began the beginning. He just exists. He just is! That's why He answered Moses when he asked Him, "Who do I say sent me?"

God said, "I AM THAT I AM. Thus shalt you say to the children of Israel, I AM have sent me unto you." For he who comes to God must believe that HE IS and that He is a rewarder of those who diligently seek Him. God created us to function like Him; we are His children. When God said, "Let there be light," and light was, that was before He created the sun. He said it, and it was. We as his children have that same ability. Let the weak say, "I am strong," and let the poor say, "I am rich." Proverbs 18:21 says, *"Death and life are in the power of the tongue, and those who love it will eat its fruit."*

We have to be careful how we choose our words when we speak about anything, especially when it comes to our own lives. The enemy knows the power you have in your tongue and uses your tongue as a weapon against you when we walk by sight such as "I'm broke"; "I'm sick"; "I'm depressed"; "I'm sick and tired"; "I can't wait"; "Why do these things always happen to me?"; etc. Then we justify it by saying, "I'm just stating the obvious or keeping it real," instead of walking by faith and not by sight. There is creative power in your tongue to cause what you see with your natural eyes to change or remain.

David understood the power in his words that it caused him to ask God. Psalm 141:3 states, *"Set a guard, O Lord, over my mouth;*

Keep watch over the door of my lips." This is one of the reasons for David's success. Just being aware alone will cause you to try and keep your words aligned with the Word. We are to cast down every thought and imagination that the enemy uses to exalt itself against the knowledge of God and to bring into captivity every thought and imagination to the obedience of Christ. Jesus demonstrated it to us when He said, "I only say what I hear My Father say." Remember when Jesus cursed the fig tree with His words for not having figs on it when He was hungry?

> *Now in the morning, as they passed by, they saw the fig tree dried up from the roots. And Peter, remembering, said to Him, "Rabbi, look! The fig tree which You cursed has withered away." So Jesus answered and said to them, "Have faith in God." For assuredly, I say to you, whoever says to this mountain, "Be removed and be cast into the sea, and does not doubt in his heart, but believes that those things he says will be done, he will have whatever he says."*
> (Mark 11:20–23)

That power will either work for you or against you, depending on the beliefs in your heart and the words you choose to let roll from your tongue. Because from the abundance of the heart, the mouth speaks.

If we don't function how God created us to function, then we are simply malfunctioning. If we don't understand what God is doing on earth and His purpose for our life or the church's purpose, then the enemy will come and, because of our lack of knowledge, fill us with his plans and purposes and use our creative power to create his plans for you and the world. The devil is a liar! When he has the church saying, "The world will get worse and worse," we believe it in our hearts because we didn't understand the passage of scripture he used against us in 2 Timothy 3 referring to that transitional generation and the end of that age. We, the church, who has the power, created the mess we have today because of misunderstanding!

Remember he tried to even temp Jesus with scripture, but Jesus didn't fall for the okey dokey but understood the ways of His Father and countered with the correct word of God. Jesus referred to that transitional generation as a wicked and adulterous generation and, thirty years later in Paul's letter to the Philippians, refers to that generation as a crooked and perverse generation. James says in chapter 3 that if we learn to bridle our tongues in the way we put a bit in the horse's mouth and cause it to go in the direction we want it to, then we can keep our lives on track.

How to function

Before the fall, we see how God related or communed with man, just walking and talking with the man in the garden in the cool of the day. The cool of the day makes it sound intimate or romantic as if there was a nice cool gentle breeze with just the right amount of leaves blowing in the air and God and man were enjoying the conversation with each other as they strolled through the beautiful garden. Then man rebels against the command of God, and God walks through the garden calling out to man, "Adam where are you?" Man being creative like his Father created the first tailor shop and made himself a green leafy double-breasted suit because he had knowledge of his nakedness. Before the fall or the rebellion, there was no sin, no heartache, no pain, no frustration, no sickness, no stress, no disagreements, only righteousness and peace and joy in the Holy Ghost. Because God is who He is, this came as no surprise. He knew man would rebel, and He already had a plan to redeem man and restore what he had lost. So God kept the details of His plan to Himself until the appointed time. Jesus makes a comment in Matthew 13:35, which reads, *"I will utter things which have been kept secret from the foundation of the world."* If we are going to be the generation that turns this mess around, then we must know what's on God's mind!

Jesus was talking to the woman at the well, who went through five husbands and had a six prospect on the line, and I want us just to look at the conclusion of that conversation.

> *But the hour is coming, and now is, when the true worshipers will worship the Father in* spirit and truth; *for the Father is seeking such to worship Him. God is Spirit, and those who worship Him* must worship in spirit and truth. (John 4:23–24; emphasis added)

We're going to have to come before Him naked and in our created nature—spirit. God is not impressed with our titles and accomplishments, or on the other hand, nothing that has to do with our flesh. Before the fall, there was no sin on earth, and God and man had nothing to hinder their relationship. But sin, God hates and can't stand it. So He sends His only begotten Son to become sin, that we might become the righteousness of God in Christ Jesus. The price of sin has been paid once and for all. There is no more need for animal sacrifices. So since they didn't get it with the veil torn in two from top to bottom, He destroyed the whole temple, and not one stone was left upon another. And the tares, or apostate Israel, was burned in the fire, and the Gentile mission stands with no opposition, now it's to whosoever will let him come.

Unfortunately, sin has left a craving in our flesh that pulls us away from God, and it always will, but the choice is simply yours to which you will serve. God is still the same as He was in the garden, for He's already said, "For I am the Lord, I change not." We are the ones who changed. We have to learn to think God's thoughts all over again. You say, "How in the world can we know what God is thinking?" I'm glad you asked. Let's look at Paul explaining how he didn't just have fancy sermons to try and persuade that wicked and perverse generation to Christ but in demonstration of the Spirit and of power. Your faith *should not be* in the wisdom of men but in the power of God.

> *However, we speak wisdom among those who are mature, yet not the wisdom of this age,* nor of the rulers of this age, who are coming to nothing. *But we speak the wisdom of God in a mystery, the hid-*

den wisdom which God ordained before the ages for our glory, which none of the rulers of this age knew; for had they known, they would not have crucified the Lord of glory. But as it is written; Eye has not seen, nor ear heard, nor have entered into the heart of man the things which God has prepared for those who love Him. But God has revealed them to us through His Spirit. *For the Spirit searches all things, yes, the deep things of God. For what man knows the things of a man except the spirit of the man which is in him? Even so no one knows the things of God except the Spirit of God. Now we have received, not the spirit of the world, but the Spirit who is from God, that we might know the things that have been freely given to us by God. These things we also speak, not in words which man's wisdom teaches but which the Holy Spirit teaches, comparing spiritual things with spiritual. But the natural man does not receive the things of the Spirit of God, for they are foolishness to him; nor can he know them, because they are spiritually discerned. But he who is spiritual judges all things, yet he himself is rightly judged by no one. For* "who has known the mind of the Lord *that he may instruct Him?"* But we have the mind of Christ. (1 Corinthians 2:6–16; emphasis added)

Only the spirit of God knows what's on God's mind, His plans for your life, the timing, the way, and everything you need to know to take your place and bring glory and honor to His name. It's all yours now. You just need to ask Him. "For it is not by might, nor by power, but by My Spirit says the Lord God Almighty!" (Zechariah 4:6). Finally, brethren, whatever things are true, whatever things are noble, whatever things are just, whatever things are pure, whatever things are lovely, whatever things are of good report, if there is any virtue and if there is anything praiseworthy, meditate on these things. This is how we commune with God—His interest becoming ours again.

Kingdom Here

Kingdom Nature

THE REASON THE church, along with the Pharisees and Zealots, have postponed the kingdom to our future is because we are looking for Jesus to come back on earth and set up a natural kingdom the way we think He should. They were looking for the Messiah to come in their day because of prophecies like Daniel 2, where he interprets Nebuchadnezzar's dream of the statute—the head of gold, which was Babylon his kingdom; the chest and arms of silver, which were the Medo-Persia; the belly and thighs of bronze, which was Greece; the legs of iron, which was Rome; and the feet of iron and clay, which was modern Europe.

Now at that time, they understood the Lord would establish His kingdom on earth because of the stone that was cut out of the mountain without hands and broke into pieces the iron, the bronze, the clay, the silver, and the gold. That stone represented the kingdom of God cut from Mt. Zion. Verse 44 says, *"And in the days of these kings, the God of heaven will set up a kingdom which shall never be destroyed; and the kingdom shall not be left to other people; it shall break in pieces and consume all these kingdoms, and it shall stand forever."*

Now when I hear some preachers teach this text, they will say that Daniel missed it or God postponed it as if Christ failed in His mission. Daniel had to go to God and ask Him what the king dreamt and what it meant because their lives depended on it. God is the one who revealed it to Daniel, and Daniel concludes by saying, "The dream is certain, and its interpretation is sure."

Remember the king didn't even remember what he had dreamed, and he was going to kill all the magicians, the astrologers, the sorcerers, and the Chaldeans unless they told him what he had dreamed and its interpretation. After the king heard Daniel, the king fell on his face, prostrate before Daniel, and commanded that they should present an offering and incense to him. Daniel got it right and told the king exactly what God had said.

The reason the Pharisees and some of our teachers today are missing it is because they're looking for Him to set up a natural or physical kingdom, and it's a spiritual kingdom. Remember those patterns I shared earlier? First, the natural and then the spiritual. First, it was Ishmael and then Isaac, Esau and then Jacob, old covenant and now new covenant, works and now faith, law and now grace, Adam and then the second Adam, Moses and then the Son of Man. Psalm 80:8 states, *"You have brought a vine out of Egypt."* Then John 15:1 says, *"I Am the True Vine."* It's with this concept that God would have you understand there's a natural Israel, a people from the loins of Abraham, Isaac, and Jacob, whose name was changed to Israel. And there is a spiritual Israel. There was the circumcision of the flesh, then the circumcision of the heart.

Let's hear what Paul was saying to the church in Rome in Romans 9:6–14.

> *But it is not that the word of God has taken no effect. For they are not all Israel who are of Israel, nor are they all children because they are the seed of Abraham; but, "In Isaac your seed shall be called." That is, those who are the children of the flesh, these are not the children of God; but the children of the promise are counted as the seed. For this is the word of promise: "At this time I will come and Sarah shall have a son." And not only this, but when Rebecca*

also had conceived by one man, even by our father Isaac for the children not yet being born, nor having done any good or evil, that the purpose of God according to election might stand, not of works but of Him who calls, it was said to her, "The older shall serve the younger." As it is written, "Jacob I have loved, but Esau I have hated."

This is what that statement refers to when Jesus says, "The last will be first and the first last." In other words, the spirit will rule the flesh in His kingdom, or the flesh shall serve the spirit and be submitted to. Now again, God is Spirit, and they who worship Him must worship Him in spirit and in truth. We walk by faith and not by sight. Remember what Jesus told Thomas, "You believe because you see, but blessed are those who believe and do not see." Jesus told Pilate that He was a king and His kingdom was not of this world. Let me close this portion out with this:

Now when He was asked by the Pharisees when the kingdom of God would come, He answered them and said, "The kingdom of God does not come with observation; nor will they say, 'See here!' or 'See there!' For Indeed, the kingdom of God is within you." (Luke 17:20–21)

So we can quit trying to interpret the Bible from the news channels, recreating the warnings and signs Jesus gave to His disciples for their generation, and be about His business for our generation.

And I bestow upon you a kingdom, just as My Father bestowed one upon Me, "that you may eat and drink at My table in My kingdom, and sit on thrones judging the twelve tribes of Israel." (Luke 22:29–30)

His plan unfolding

God, because He is who He is—the Alpha and Omega; the Beginning and the End; the First and the Last; omniscient, all-knowing; omnipotence, all-powerful; omnipresent, everywhere at once! This is why He chooses to start at the end before He begins. He doesn't make these things up as we go. This is the language we hear from Him, He foreknew or predestined. These types of phrases are there to let you know that God has already been there and done that! You can't surprise God. He's already made a way for you before you ever needed Him to make a way. He said in Jeremiah 1:5, *"Before I formed you in the womb I knew you; Before you were born I sanctified you; I ordained you a prophet to the nation."*

God was telling Jeremiah, "I already did it. I already made a way even if it seems like there is no way, just trust that my will on earth for you has an expected end because I ended it before I started it." When they were taken by Babylon into captivity, God encourages him again in verse 29:11, *"For I know the thoughts that I think toward you, says the Lord, thoughts of peace and not of evil, to give you a future and a hope."* He's telling Jeremiah, "This is not how your story ends."

Mysteries and secrets—make no mistake about it. God is awesome at keeping secrets or hiding things, to the point that you can go through your whole life not knowing who you are, let alone knowing the fullness of who He is. So when God told the devil in the garden with Adam that He already fixed this mess he made and just gave him the end result, he said, "I will bruise My heel with your head." All the devil knew was there was a serious kick or stomping in his future, but he didn't know when or how. So here's a quick overview of God's plan on earth after the fall of man.

> *Therefore, just as through one man sin entered the world, and death through sin, and thus death spread to all men, because all sinned. For until the law sin was in the world, but sin is not imputed when there is no law. Nevertheless, death reigned from Adam to Moses, even over those who had not*

> *sinned according to the likeness of the transgression*
> *of Adam, who is a type of Him who was to come.*
> (Romans 5:12–14; emphasis added)

Then God made a promise to Abraham that He would make a great nation out of him. Then came Isaac, then Jacob, whose name was changed to Israel, and his twelve sons became the people of God also known as *the Jewish mission*. The Jewish mission did not come to a complete end until AD 70. But Isaiah 9:6–7 states,

> *For unto us a Child is born, unto us a Son is given;*
> *and the government will be upon His shoulder.*
> *And His name will be called Wonderful, Counselor,*
> *Mighty God, Everlasting Father, Prince of Peace. Of*
> *the Increase of His government and peace there will*
> *be no end, upon the throne of David and over His*
> *kingdom, to order it and establish it with judgment*
> *and justice from that time forward, even forever.*
> *The zeal of the Lord of hosts will perform this.*

Now Jesus is on the planet to do the will of His Father and that was not just to die for us so we can go to heaven. That's what religion taught us. In fact, He didn't bring a religion at all but the government of heaven to earth. Luke 16:16 says, *"The law and the prophets were until John. Since that time the* kingdom of God *has been preached, and everyone is pressing into it."* God's purpose is to bring His government to the earth, and the church is trying to get off the earth. Jesus came to redeem man, restore our relationship with the Father, bring the kingdom of heaven to earth, reinstate the Adamic authority man lost (dominion), and return the Holy Spirit back to man on earth—the power to build God's kingdom and His culture through His children by His Spirit and the kingdom of heavens' influence on the earth. In AD 30–34, Jesus did the will of His Father and sent the Holy Spirit and birthed the Gentile mission through His disciples.

In Ephesians 3:1–6—I will paraphrase verses 1–5 because it's verse 6 I'm after—Paul said he was a prisoner of Christ Jesus for the

Gentiles. How, by revelation, was made known to him the *mystery* that had not been made known to men in other ages? "That the Gentiles should be fellow heirs, of the same body, and partakers of His promise in Christ through the gospel." Paul was saying that God had revealed to him that the Gentiles would be fellow heirs and we see in Acts 10 and 11 the other disciples coming to this revelation through Peter. This is why we need to understand this transitional generation because we have the Jewish mission. To the Jew first coming to an end but still alive until AD 70 and the Gentile mission beginning, this is what Paul meant in his letter to the Corinthians when he said he is an apostle born out of season because even though he was an apostle to the Gentiles, he still had to go to the Jews first. Now that the Gentile mission is in full effect, I'll let Daniel close this portion out when he sees the first year of King Darius and what would be accomplished at that time.

> *In the first year of his reign, I, Daniel, understood by the books the number of the years specified by the word of the Lord through Jeremiah the prophet, that He would accomplish* seventy years *in the desolations of Jerusalem.*
>
> *Seventy weeks are determined for your people and for your holy city, to finish the transgression, to make an end of sins, to make reconciliation for iniquity, to bring in everlasting righteousness, to seal up vision and prophecy, and to anoint the Most Holy. Know therefore and understand, that from the going forth of the command to restore and build Jerusalem until Messiah the Prince, there shall be seven weeks and sixty-two weeks; The street shall be built again, and the wall, even in troublesome times. And after the sixty-two weeks Messiah shall be cut off, but not for Himself; And the people of the prince who is to come* shall destroy the city and the sanctuary. *The end of it shall be with a flood, and till the end of the war desolations are determined. Then he shall*

> *confirm a covenant with many for one week; But in the middle of the week, he shall bring an end to sacrifice and offering. And on the wing of abominations shall be one who makes desolate, even until the consummation, which is determined, is poured out on the desolate.* (Daniel 9:2, 24–27; emphasis added)

The remnant

We just took a look at what God had been doing on earth since Adam and the fall of man, working His plan that He had in mind from the foundation of the earth—a plan that He did not share fully with man nor the enemy but kept it a secret unto Himself until He decided it's time, leaving it a mystery for thousands of years to us, but to Him a few days. No man has God all figured out, and no single man ever will. The moment you think you have a handle on Him, He reveals to you another layer that blows your mind. Do you remember what happened to Moses when he asked God if he could see Him? God told Moses, "You can't handle seeing Me in My fullness, your mind could not contain all that I AM." But He placed him in the cleft of the rock and let Moses see His back as He passed by. Moses's head lit up like a thousand-watt light bulb for months to the place where the people were afraid to even look at Moses, so he covered his head to continue his work.

Paul said we see in part and we prophesy in part, but the only one who knows it all is the spirit of God, which now abides in you. God has always been on a mission on earth with the goal of filling the earth with His glory through His children. Habakkuk 2:14 says, *"For the earth will be filled with the knowledge of the glory of the Lord, as the waters cover the sea."* We see His work in the Old Testament on how He made a covenant with the Jews to make a distinction between His people and the people who were not in covenant with Him, known as the Gentiles.

Then God, before He went silent for four hundred years, left man with another promise in Malachi 3:1 that reads, *"Behold, I send my messenger, and he will prepare the way before Me. And the Lord, whom you seek, will suddenly come to His temple, even the Messenger of the covenant, in whom you delight. Behold, He is coming, says the Lord of hosts."*

Now John showed up in the wilderness preaching repentance for the kingdom of God is near. Jesus came and began to preach the kingdom of God and told us all the law and the prophets were until John, but since then, the kingdom of God has been preached. Now God was about to do a new thing on earth, where old things were passing away and all things were becoming new. This was the introduction of the transitional generation, all technically still under the Jewish mission, which was coming to an end in AD 70. The dawn of the Gentile mission was being birthed to whosoever may come—a new creation.

I explained why so many have missed it by looking for the promises of God to be fulfilled naturally. God was still working His plan on earth through certain people to keep His purpose on earth moving His way and not man's. Let's let Paul explain here as he quotes Isaiah in Romans 9:27–33 (emphasis added).

> *Isaiah also cries out concerning Israel:* "Though the number of the children of Israel be as the sand of the sea, *the remnant will be saved. For He will finish the work and cut it short in righteousness, because the Lord will make a short work upon the earth." And as Isaiah said before:* "Unless the Lord of Sabaoth had left us *a seed, we would have become like Sodom, and we would have been made like Gomorrah." What shall we say then?* That Gentiles, *who did not pursue righteousness,* have attained *to righteousness, even the righteousness of faith;* but Israel, *pursuing the law of righteousness,* has not attained *to the law of righteousness.* Why? *Because they did not seek it* by faith, *but as it were,* by the works *of the law. For they stumbled at the stumbling stone. As it is written:* "Behold, I lay in

Zion a stumbling stone and rock of offense, and whoever believes on Him will not be put to shame."

This transition from the old covenant to the new covenant in the way God had planned from the foundation of the earth to perform it on earth is one of the mysteries of God unfolding right before them, and they didn't have a clue because they chose to hold to their traditions or their own understanding. They would reject Jesus and say, "We're Moses's disciples," and kill the prophets, God's Son, and His disciples.

It's crucial for us today to understand these events so that we might understand what God is doing on earth today and find the purpose for our lives in His grand scheme of things. Let's close this portion with Paul once again explaining these events in Romans 11:1–8 (emphasis added).

I say then, has God cast away His people? Certainly not! For I also am an Israelite, of the seed of Abraham, of the tribe of Benjamin. God has not cast away his people whom He foreknew. Or do you not know what the scripture says of Elijah, how he pleads with God against Israel, saying, "Lord, they have killed Your prophets and torn down Your altars, and I alone am left, and they seek my life?" But what does the divine response say to him? "I have reserved for Myself seven thousand men who have not bowed the knee to Baal." Even so then, at this present time there is a remnant according to the election of grace. And if by grace, then it is no longer of works, otherwise grace is no longer grace. But if it is of works, it is no longer grace; otherwise work is no longer work. What then? Israel has not obtained what it seeks; but the elect have obtained it, and the rest were blinded. Just as it is written: "God has given them a spirit of stupor, eyes that they should not see and ears that they should not hear, to this very day."

What was it that Israel sought and did not obtain? The kingdom of God! They knew it was coming, but they did not know how. They did not know that the King would come lying in a manger, wrapped in swaddling clothing, die on a cross, rise again three days later with the keys of death, hell, and the grave, and be seated at the right hand of the Father with all power and authority given to Him reigning as King of kings and Lord of lords. Not a clue! One more verse states, *"For I do not desire, brethren, that you should be ignorant of* this mystery, *lest you should be wise in your own opinion,* that blindness in part *has happened to Israel* until the fullness of the Gentiles *has come in."* That said it all right there for you to see the work being done in that generation until the fullness of the Gentile mission had come in, which it did in AD 70. So can we move forward and be about our Father's business on earth today and enhance the kingdom of God?

CHAPTER 8

Kingdom Restored

New Creation

REMEMBER THIS FACT: To His kingdom, there would be no end! It will never be destroyed, and it will consume all other kingdoms or governments that would come against it (Daniel 2:44). God tells us not to despise the day of small beginnings because He knows how He does things. His ways are not our ways, but in order for us to do His will on the earth, we need to repent, change the way we think, and make our ways line up with His ways. God started the human race with one man and told him to be fruitful and multiply. In the same way, God has started a new creation with one man, and for man to become part of the new creation, he must be born again, which restores our citizenship in heaven. When God told Adam, "The day you eat from this tree you shall surely die," we know God did not mean physically, or else, Adam would have dropped dead after one bite. What Adam lost was sonship with the heavenly Father. Therefore, he was cut off completely from the kingdom of God and lost all access and authority given to him by God. He became dead to God in his sin.

Sin separates you from God, and the wages of sin are death. The spirit of God immediately left man, which cut off heaven's power and influence on man, and man was left to be governed by a different law and system—the law of sin and death, which is Satan's law, now influenced by the flesh because of his rebellion to his heavenly Father. So Adam, still created in the image of God but not being influenced by God, is now having to adapt to his surroundings by use of his five senses and adjusting to this foreign law of sin and death, which is the lust of the flesh, the lust of the eye, and the pride of life. First John 2:16 says, *"For all that is in the world—the lust of the flesh, the lust of the eyes, and the pride of life—is not of the Father but is of the world."* So when Adam and Eve knew each other and began to be fruitful and multiply, their seed had now become sinful, and they produced after their kind. Therefore, everyone was born into sin and death, separated from the heavenly Father, and so was the earth's population. But God so loved the man that He had created and missed His strolls in the garden in the cool of the day, that He kept His plan to redeem man and restore unto him what he had lost a secret from Satan because it was none of his business, and even man, because he was no longer capable of handling the truth.

First Corinthians 2:14 says, *"But the natural man does not receive the things of the Spirit of God, for they are foolishness to him; nor can he know them, because they are spiritually discerned"* (emphasis added). God's plan was always to redeem man from the enemy and restore the kingdom back to man, and when Jesus had become sin, taking our place on the cross, which separated Him from the Father, we heard Jesus say, "My God, My God, why have you forsaken Me?" He pays the price for sin in full, enters hell for three days, and comes back with the keys of death, hell, and the grave, and the saints of old Abraham, Isaac, Jacob, David, and the prophets, just to name a few.

> *Then, behold, the veil of the temple was torn in two* from top to bottom; *and the earth quaked, and the rocks were split, and the* graves *were opened; and* many bodies *of the saints who had fallen asleep were raised; and coming out of the graves after His resurrection, they went into the holy city and appeared to many.* (Matthew 27:51–53; emphasis added)

God was the first to leave no saint behind! Had the enemy known God's secret, he would not have crucified the Lord of glory and we would still be dead in our trespasses and sins and dead to God.

> *And you He made alive, who were dead in trespasses and sins, in which you once walked according to the course of this world, according to the prince of the power of the air, the spirit who now works in the sons of disobedience, among whom also we all once conducted ourselves in the lusts of our flesh, fulfilling the desires of the flesh and of the mind, and* were by nature *children of wrath, just as the others.* But God, *who is rich in mercy, because of His great love with which He loved us, even when we were dead in trespasses, made us alive together with Christ [*by grace you have been saved*], and raised us up together, and made us sit together in the heavenly places in Christ Jesus, that in* the ages to come *He might show the exceeding riches of His grace in His kindness toward us in Christ Jesus.* (Ephesians 2:1–7; emphasis added)

Now it is a must that I have you look for yourselves so you can see how God has restored the kingdom relationship along with its power and authority as it was in the garden by the statements Paul made in verse 6. He raised us together and seated us together in Christ Jesus. Where have we been seated with Christ? Go back a few verses to see where we have been seated with Him in chapter 1:21–23 (emphasis added),

> *Far above all principality and power and might and dominion, and every name that is named, not only in this age but also in that which is to come. And He put all things under His feet, and gave Him to*

be Head over all things to the church, *which is His body, the fullness of Him who fills all in all.*

The second Adam, which is Christ, has restored the Adamic authority to the church and settled the bill due for sin once and for all. *Paid in full!*

Attitude of gratitude

God is still moving on earth today, and He is exposing the mysteries and secrets He kept hidden in Himself from the foundation of the world. He absolutely revealed these things to the early church with so much opposition against them that they wrote these letters to the churches in a spirit of desperation or admonishing the other churches because they understood the mission that Jesus left them with. They also understood it had a clock on it. I doubt very seriously that they were asking God for big houses and good jobs when they knew that they were being killed for His name's sake.

Paul and the disciples were resilient in their endeavor, pressing toward the mark of the high calling of God through real trials and rejoicing when they were beaten, stoned, imprisoned, and writing letters to the churches, telling them to count it all joy when going through their trials and tribulations. Paul was warned about what would happen to him if he went to Rome and his response was that he was ready to die for the gospel's sake. The opposition that Jesus faced while He visited the earth didn't stop because He left, but it grew worse. Peter was crucified upside down because he told the soldiers he wasn't worthy to die like his Savior. The kingdom of God continued to suffer violence, but the violence took it by force without carnal weapons. Paul was the one who wrote in those times, mostly from a jail cell, that the weapons of our warfare are not carnal; but they are mighty to the pulling down of strongholds, telling the church to put on the whole armor of God so that they may be able to stand against the wiles of the enemy. When he decided to let them kill him, he was sure to let the church know he had finished his course and he fought a good fight, by faith!

Let's look at Paul's second letter to the church in Corinth, and you can hear Paul's resiliency in his mission and what he thought about those who opposed him for His name's sake.

> *Are they Hebrews? So am I. Are they Israelites? So am I. Are they the seed of Abraham? So am I. Are they ministers of Christ?—I speak as a fool—I am more: in labors more abundant, in stripes above measure, in prisons more frequently, in deaths often. From the Jews five times I received forty stripes minus one. Three times I was beaten with rods; once I was stoned; three times I was shipwrecked; a night and a day I have been in the deep; in journeys often, in perils of water, in perils of robbers, in perils of my own countrymen, in perils of the Gentiles, in perils in the city, in perils in the wilderness, in perils in the sea, in perils among false brethren; in weariness and toil, in sleeplessness often, in hunger and thirst, in fastings often, in cold and nakedness—besides the other things, what comes upon me daily:* my deep concern *for all the churches. Who is weak, and I am not weak? Who is made to stumble, and I do not burn with indignation? If I must boast, I will boast in the things which concern my infirmity. The God and Father of our Lord Jesus Christ, who is blessed forever, knows that I am not lying. In Damascus the governor, under Aretas the king, was guarding the city of the Damascenes with a garrison, desiring to arrest me; but I was let down in a basket through a window in the wall, and escaped from his hands.* (2 Corinthians 11:22–33; emphasis added)

If you didn't just get checked by Paul's journey, you are reading too fast! Can you imagine what his back looked like after being on the Romans' whipping post five times? Some historians say that Paul looked weird because he had a crooked nose and walked with a limp.

Could it have been because he had been beaten three times with rods or maybe when he was stoned? Not to mention his perils and serious and immediate dangers. Their deep concerns were only to finish the task that Jesus had entrusted them with. Many times in their letters they would mention us when they would say, "Not only for this age but for the age to come."

Just think about where we would be had they lived their lives like today's average Christian—no concern about what God is doing on earth, just gimme this and gimme that, and I'll be sure to give you the praise. Our time is our time, and we do what we feel like doing when we feel like doing it. We would be lost if they would have taken that approach—just as long as I go to heaven, I'm good. We must do better to get better results for the mission that God has assigned to our generation and not for our generation alone but for the generations to come.

Remember what Jesus said in Matthew 5:20: *"For I say to you, that unless your righteousness* exceeds *the righteousness of the scribes and Pharisees, you will by* no means *enter the kingdom of heaven."* We, the church, must consider our ways! A kingdom divided against itself will not stand! We have allowed the enemy to set his barriers all throughout the body of Christ, and many of us have been busy with our own agendas and not God's. Racism, socialism, classism, denominationalism, sexism—if we don't clean up our act, by no means, will we enter the kingdom of heaven!

> *Therefore we also, since we are surrounded by so great a cloud of witnesses,* let us *lay aside every weight, and the sin which so easily* ensnares us, *and let us run with endurance the race that is set before us, looking unto Jesus, the author and finisher of our faith, who for the joy that was set before Him endured the cross, despising the shame, and* has sat down *at the right hand of the throne of God. For* consider Him *who endured such hostility from sinners against Himself, lest you become weary and discouraged in your souls. You have not yet resisted to*

bloodshed, striving against sin. (Hebrews 12:1–4; emphasis added)

How good and pleasant it will be when the body of Christ decides to live together in unity. The gates of hell would not stand a chance because greater is He that lives in us than he that operates the world's system.

Ministry of Reconciliation

What is God doing on earth today? For God so loved the world that He gave His only Son a mission to take the government of heaven to earth, become sin to take man's place, die on a cross, and shed His blood to usher in a new covenant and to pay for man's sin in full. He sends the Holy Spirit to fill the temple that will not be made by hands and Him being the cornerstone, then puts His word in their hearts, and fills the earth with the knowledge of the kingdom and the glory of the Lord as the waters cover the sea. This is the new creation of God, and it is now available to whosoever! God loves the world. That means everybody—straight or the A–Z community, black, white, red, brown, beige, gray, prejudiced, hateful, Christians, Muslims, Hindus, Buddhists, pimps, prostitutes, presidents, governors, thieves, murderers, blind, cripples, crazy, the IRS, the police, and you too. Whosoever! There's not a sinner or soul on this earth that the blood of Jesus didn't atone for, and God wants His kids back! God is reconciling the world to Himself through the body of Christ, which is the church.

> *You are the salt of the earth; but if the salt loses its flavor, how shall it be seasoned? It is then good for nothing but to be thrown out and trampled under foot by men. You are the light of the world. A city that is set on a hill cannot be hidden. Nor do they light a lamp and put it under a basket, but on a lampstand, and it gives light to all who are in the house. Let your light so shine before men, that they*

may see your good works and glorify your Father in heaven. (Matthew 5:13–16; emphasis added)

This sounds like the Lord expects us to bring change to a lost world. He said *we are the salt* of the earth. I've never put salt on my food without it changing the taste immediately. He said *we are the light* of the world. Have you ever walked into a dark room and turned on the light and darkness decided to hang around? Well, He's saying that's how it would be if we obeyed His commands. This is our job, not His! He does not have us here on earth to call ourselves standing in the gap and telling Him to go and change situations that He's showing you to go and be that agent of change. The problem is that disobedience causes you to lose your flavor and then you are good for nothing but to be thrown out and trampled under the foot of men. That is where many Christians choose to live their lives.

> *Therefore, if anyone is in Christ,* he is a new creation; *old thing have passed away; behold; all things have become new. Now all things are of God, who has reconciled us to Himself through Jesus Christ, and* has given us *the ministry of reconciliation, that is, that God was in Christ reconciling the world to Himself,* not imputing *their trespasses to them, and has* committed to us *the word of reconciliation. Now then,* we are ambassadors *for Christ, as though God were pleading through us: we implore you on Christ's behalf, be reconciled to God.* (2 Corinthians 5:17–20; emphasis added)

We will never be able to manifest the new creation in our flesh. There's no half-in and half-out. It's either you are in or you are out, only by His spirit and us fulfilling the two greatest commandments—to love God with all your heart and your soul and your mind and your neighbor as yourself. An ambassador's goal is to influence the territory of his country—in this case, the kingdom of heaven. God has demonstrated to us when He gave His only Son to die in our place what He values the most. Religion was not God's plan to fix the problems on earth. It was to help equip the saints to become His ambassadors for Christ who would represent heaven's culture on earth. Thy kingdom come, thy will be done, on earth as it is in heaven! Influence to bring change with the love of God flowing out of your belly like rivers of living water. When God strategically places us on our jobs, in our families, in our communities, and in churches with friends, we should be walking and talking with the Holy Spirit to see what it is He wants us to do or learn in our assigned territory, especially when it's challenging for you to be there. He always has His reasons. Kingdom culture does not function like the world, and you are placed to represent heaven in a lost world.

> *You have heard that it was said, "You shall love your neighbor and hate your enemy." But I say to you, love your enemies, bless those who curse you, do good to those who hate you, and pray for those who spitefully use you and persecute you,* that you may be *sons of your Father in heaven; for He makes His sun rise on the evil and on the good, and sends rain on the just and on the unjust. For if you love those who love you, what reward have you? Do not even the tax collectors do the same? And if you greet your brethren only, what do you do more than others? Do not even the tax collectors do so? Therefore, you shall be perfect, just as your Father in heaven is perfect.* (Matthew 5:43–48; emphasis added)

Jesus is saying that He has not sent you to look and act as the world does but to look and act like your Father, who is in heaven, and you will be perfect. Your light will shine, and your salt will have its flavor, and you will be like yeast that God has placed in dough until the whole lump has become yeast.

CHAPTER 9

Kingdom Positions

Ambassadors and King

IN THE PASSAGE we just looked at, Paul said that we are ambassadors for Christ. Earlier, I had mentioned that Jesus's earthly ministry was as an ambassador. He would make statements like "I only say what I hear My Father say" and "I only do what I see My Father do." His ministry was Him representing His heavenly Father and a heavenly kingdom in His walk on earth. I was sure to say in His ministry that He was here on a specific assignment and did not receive His kingdom until the ascension to the Father.

> *I was watching in the night visions, and behold,
> One like the Son of Man, coming with the clouds of
> heaven! He came to the Ancient of Days, and they
> brought Him near before Him. Then to Him was
> given dominion and glory and a kingdom, That all
> peoples, nations, and languages should serve Him.
> His dominion is an everlasting dominion, which
> shall not pass away, and His kingdom the one
> which shall not be destroyed.* (Daniel 7:13–14;
> emphasis added)

This was the joy that the Lord chose to focus on that enabled Him to endure the cross. Knowing His Father is faithful to His promises, He remained faithful to His earthly assignment in representing His Father through all the opposition the scribes and Pharisees brought against Him.

> *Why do the nations rage, and the people plot a vain thing? The kings of the earth set themselves, and the rulers take counsel together,* against the Lord *and* against His Anointed, *saying, "Let us break their bonds in pieces and cast away their cords from us."* *He who sits in the heavens shall laugh; the Lord shall hold them in derision. Then He shall speak to them in His wrath, and distress them in His deep displeasure:* [Olivet Discourse] *"Yet I have set My King on My holy hill of Zion."* I will declare the decree: *The Lord has said to me, You are My Son, today I have begotten You. Ask of Me, and I will* give You the nations *for Your inheritance, and* the ends of the earth for Your possession. (Psalm 2:1–8; emphasis added)

Verses 9–12 refer to the destruction of Jerusalem in AD 70 with the only two choices: *kiss the Son*, receive Him and His message; or *perish*, receive His judgment.

> *I came to send fire on the earth, and how I wish it were already kindled! But I have a baptism to be baptized with, and* how distressed I am till it is accomplished! (Luke 12:49–50; emphasis added)

God in verse 7 of Psalm 2 said, "I will declare the decree," and that decree of when He would set His King upon His holy hill of Zion was, *"You are My Son, today I have begotten You."* Now if in the beginning was the Word and the Word was with God and the Word was God, then we know that the Word, which is His Son, did not begin with Jesus's birth through Mary. So the Son has never been separated from the Father in all eternity for the Father to be able to say to His Son, "Today I have begotten thee," except the time He was separated from the Father—when He became sin on the cross and took our place and went to hell on our behalf and asked His Father on the cross, "Why have you forsaken Me?" The definition of *forsaken* is "abandoned" or "deserted." God is holy, and the moment Jesus became sin upon that cross, God left Jesus because there is no sin in Him! But Jesus had the decree!

> God has fulfilled this *for us their children, in that He has raised up Jesus. As it is also written in the* second Psalms*: "You are my Son, Today I have begotten You." And that He raised Him from the dead, no more to return to corruption, He has spoken thus.* (Acts 13:33–34; emphasis added)

Now King Jesus has appointed us as ambassadors in His kingdom with the ministry of reconciliation, with the promise remaining that God will give Him the nations for His inheritance and the ends of the earth for His possession! His kingdom is an everlasting kingdom, and it shall not be destroyed. Therefore, the teaching that tells us He will come and set up a natural kingdom in Jerusalem and lock up the devil for a thousand years and there will be peace on the earth gives the impression that God has to remove the devil for His Son to reign as King on earth. Not true!

> *The Lord said to my Lord, "Sit at My right hand, till I make Your enemies Your footstool." The Lord shall send the rod of Your strength out of Zion.* Rule in the midst of Your enemies! (Psalm 110:1–2; emphasis added)

Jesus is King right now, reigning among His enemies until all His enemies are made a footstool for His feet. Now that does not sound like we should be using the power that has been given to us by believing and confessing that the world will get worse and worse but getting in agreement with the King for He's coming back for a victorious church without a spot, blemish, or wrinkle.

> *Behold, is it not of the Lord of hosts that the peoples labor to feed the fire, and* nations *weary themselves in vain? For the earth will be filled with the knowledge of the glory of the Lord, as the water covers the sea.* (Habakkuk 2:13–14; emphasis added)

The worst and worst passages were speaking of that transitional generation, and that's all behind us. For verse 21 in Matthew 24, it says that it never shall be again. Let's close this portion with Paul speaking on the matter in 1 Corinthians 15:20–28.

> But now Christ is risen from the dead, *and has become the first fruits of those who have fallen asleep. For since by man came death, by Man also came the resurrection of the dead. For as in Adam all die, even so in Christ all shall be made alive. But each one in his own order: Christ the first fruits, afterward those who are Christ's at His coming. Then comes the end, when He delivers the kingdom to God the Father, when He puts an end to all rule and all authority and power.* For He must reign till *He has put all enemies under His feet.* The last enemy *that will be destroyed* is death. *For He has put all things under His feet. But when He says all things are under Him,* it is evident *that He who put all things under Him* is excepted. *Now when all things are made subject to Him, then the Son Himself will also be subject to Him who put all things under Him, that God maybe all in all.* (Emphasis added)

Therefore, Jesus is not coming back to establish His kingdom but to consummate His kingdom. The definition of *consummate* is showing a high degree of skill and flair; complete or perfect. For example, "She's dressed with *consummate* elegance." The bride will be ready for His return, the Holy Ghost is here to make sure of it!

Ambassadors for Christ

Why ambassadors? If we take a look at some of the characteristics of an ambassador and how one represents his country, then it will help us understand what the King expects from us. The first thing we must understand if we're going to fulfill His will on earth is that when we are born again and made alive to God again, *our citizenship is in heaven* even though being still here on earth is a sign that God is not finished with the work He has in store for us here. We're in this world but not of this world. He's not looking for dual citizenship. He has us here to represent heaven on earth. That is why we must learn the culture of heaven, which is the very thing Jesus was teaching. For example, in the kingdom of heaven, we love our enemies, we bless those who curse us, we do good to those who hate us, and we pray for those who lie to us and persecute us for no reason. Remember all that Paul said he went through? It was his love for Christ and his love for the people that He assigned to him that caused him to press on. Those are the two greatest commandments at work.

When we understand our citizenship is in heaven and not on earth, as an ambassador for the kingdom of heaven, we have diplomatic immunity—a status that is granted to us as a diplomat that exempts us from the laws of a foreign jurisdiction. This is how Paul and Silas were able to send praises unto their King, who was in heaven, and it shook the ground where they stood and freed all the prisoners. And they did not even have to try to run. You, as an ambassador, are appointed by the King. Remember, a kingdom is not a democracy. The power is not with the people in a kingdom. The King has all the power, and when He appoints you, it is settled! An ambassador is only committed to his country's interest. He or she embodies their nation or kingdom. When you see them, you will be looking at the whole kingdom and not a person. Jesus would always say upon His arrival that the kingdom of God is here. Romans 14:17 states, *"For the kingdom of God is not eating and drinking, but righteousness and peace and joy in the Holy Spirit."*

Remember Luke 17:20–21 says,

> *Now when He was asked by the Pharisees when the kingdom of God will come, He answered them and said, "The kingdom of God does not come with observation; nor will they say, 'See here!' or 'See there!' For indeed,* the kingdom of God is within you.*"* (Emphasis added)

That means every day, every moment, while you sleep, while you creep, the kingdom of God is in you, and the King expects you to represent. An ambassador is only authorized to speak their government's position and never their personal opinion. For example, you may be asked, "What do you think about homosexuality?" Your response should be, "My government's position is, it is an abomination." No democracy. If the King says it's an abomination, then it's an abomination. He didn't ask you for your opinion on the matter, and He never will. He is King, not president. But to be clear, we are commanded to love the sinner but not the sin. An ambassador is totally covered by his government. In other words, the King does not want you to get distracted by personal needs or wants. All your needs are met according to His riches in glory when you seek first the kingdom of God and His righteousness, and all the things you want and need will be added unto you. You have total access to your government's wealth and power. An ambassador who has his country's full military might be backing him or her. Vengeance belongs to God!

> *Beloved, do not avenge yourselves,* but rather give place to wrath; *for it is written, "Vengeance is Mine, I will repay," says the Lord. Therefore "If your enemy is hungry, feed him; If he is thirsty, give him a drink; For in so doing you will heap coals*

of fire on his head." Do not be overcome by evil, but overcome evil with good. (Romans 12:19–21; emphasis added)

An ambassador always stays in constant contact and communication with their government, and their main goal is to influence the territory they are assigned to for their government. Well, I believe it is safe to say that an ambassador can be likened to some salt or light and should be an agent of change for the glory of their country—an ambassador's position as the king of God can only be recalled by the King. Remember, His grace is sufficient for you. A righteous man may fall seven times a day and get back up, but grace is not a license to sin but covers you when you make mistakes. Remember, Jesus did not bring to earth a religion, but a government was upon His shoulders. Our lives are not our own. We have been bought with a price, and the King owns everything, including you. We are just stewards of the King's possessions; the earth is the Lord and the fullness thereof. Now I will finish this portion with a warning from the King found in Matthew 18:6–7.

But whoever causes one of these little ones who believe in Me to sin, it would be better for him if a millstone were hung around his neck, and he were drowned in the depth of the sea. Woe to the world because of offense! For offenses must come, but woe to that man by whom the offenses come!

I said that the word *ambassador* should give us an idea of what the Lord's expectation is from His believers.

Therefore, come out from among them and be separate, says the Lord. Do not touch what is unclean, and I will receive you. I will be a Father to you, and you shall be My sons and daughters, says the Lord Almighty. (2 Corinthians 6:17–18)

Conquering the wilderness

When God created you, He had a specific purpose in mind for you to fulfill in your lifetime here on earth. Jesus said if you find your life, you will lose it, but if you lose your life for His sake, you will find it. This statement is a matter of you making your personal decision to die to yourself or take up your cross on a daily basis and follow Him. His way will not be your way, and His thoughts will not be your thoughts. God will not change His ways to come in agreement with the way you see things or submit to your understanding and allow you to receive your inheritance by grace. He knows who He is. He's the King, not us.

Salvation is given to you by His grace, and once you are born again, your heavenly Father begins to teach you who you are now. Even though you are a baby Christian, He knows and understands exactly where you are in the predestined journey He has prepared for you. Can you remember when you first got saved and prayed to your new heavenly Father and He would answer your prayers quickly to let you know He was there? Just like a parent taking home their newborn child, all they have to do is cry, and we start grabbing pacifiers, filling bottles, checking diapers, picking them up, and rocking them while you sing or hum the old classic lullabies. Yeah, He knows what time it is with His children, and He is a good Father who does chasten those He loves.

Now you know when that season is over, God is expecting you to grow up. When the prayers stop being answered so quickly, God is teaching you to quit crying and start talking and walking with Him. The dirty diapers are not cute anymore. There are two things I want you to get from this concept, and the first is the reason why Jesus only revealed Himself along with the secrets and mysteries of the gospel to the twelve disciples. He was not planning on staying on earth in His physical form forever. Establishing a natural kingdom on the earth was not His plan even though that's how man read into it. For they had no clue about His plan to come and die, or as the Bible says, they would not have crucified the Lord of glory. The second thing is that the purpose of the fivefold ministry is for the training up of the new man so that he may grow up and receive his inheritance. Israel wandered in the wilderness for forty years in this very process of repentance that their minds be renewed. It's one thing to raise and train a child from birth, but raising a child from birth who has aged in another form and has to learn to put off the old man with his old ways of thinking and the new birth being in a new nature—that is not visible to the natural eye—will take Jesus Himself and the five-fold ministry, along with trials set up by the Father and you being filled and led by His spirit to get you to mature. Paul was explaining this to the church in Ephesus when he wrote in Ephesians 4:17–32,

> *This I say, therefore, and testify in the Lord, that you should no longer walk as the rest of the Gentiles walk, in the futility of their mind, having their understanding darkened,* being alienated from the life of God, *because of the ignorance that is in them, because of the blindness of their hearts; who, being past feeling, have given themselves over to lewdness, to work all uncleanness with greediness.* But you have not so learned Christ, *if indeed you have heard Him and have been taught by Him, as the truth is in Jesus:* that you put off, *concerning your former conduct,* the old man *which grows corrupt according to the deceitful lusts,* and be renewed *in the spirit of your mind, and that you* put on the new man *which was created according to God, in true righteousness and holiness. Therefore, putting away lying,* "Let each one of you speak truth with his neighbor," *for we are members of one another. Be angry, and do not sin: do not let the sun go down on your wrath, nor give place to the devil. Let him who stole steal no longer, but rather let him labor, working with his hands what is good,* that he may have something to give *him who has need. Let no corrupt word proceed out of your mouth, but what is good for necessary edification,* that it may

impart grace *to the hearer. And do not grieve the Holy Spirit of God, by whom you were sealed for the day of redemption. Let all bitterness, wrath, anger, clamor, and evil speaking* be put away from you, *with all malice.* And be kind *to one another, tenderhearted, forgiving one another, even as God in Christ forgave you.* (Emphasis added)

When we learn to put the old natural man of the flesh on the cross daily ourselves and put on the new man of the spirit and the characteristics of our heavenly Father become dominant in our lives, then the work of the wilderness does come to an end, and God will allow you to possess your inheritance. He said for you to enter the kingdom of God, you must become a little child in your natural man—not as an adult because adults want to negotiate and not as a teenager because they think they got it all figured out, but a little child. They simply obey and love one another, making you ready to go in and possess the land.

CHAPTER 10

Kingdom Enhancement

Kingdom Accountability

FOR US TO successfully enhance the kingdom of God, we have to begin to view ourselves how God sees us, and He sees us as a whole. When God had finished His work in the wilderness with the people of Israel and finally had them with one mind and on one accord, they began to possess the land, and the promise of God started to become their reality. God had given them a miraculous victory against Jericho as their tremendous fortified walls that surrounded Jericho came down with a shout from the nation of Israel as God had commanded.

The people of Israel had heard how God brought the generation before them out of Egypt with a mighty hand and destroyed all their enemies as they wandered around the wilderness. But now firsthand as they began to enter the promised land, they could see God moving in a mighty way on their behalf. The people became excited and knew they could not lose with God on their side. They were ready to go after the thirty kingdoms that remained. But they came up on Ai, which was a lesser opponent than Jericho, and they assumed to have a quick and easy victory over them. And Ai started whooping Israel, and twelve thousand men and women fell that day because of Achan—one man's disobedience out of millions of them. Joshua was stunned, and the people of Israel were now afraid because of the defeat and catastrophe at Ai. God said it like this, "But the children of Israel committed a trespass *regarding the accursed things, for Achan of the tribe of Judah, took of the accursed things; so the anger of the Lord burned against* the children of Israel."

Achan took a Babylonian garment and buried it under his tent, and the Lord saw it. The nation of Israel committed a trespass, not Achan committed a trespass. After Joshua sought the Lord on the outcome and God revealed to Joshua who did what, the Lord went on to say, *"Neither will I be with you anymore* unless *you destroy the accursed from among you."* So Joshua confronted Achan, gathered up him, his family, his animals, and all his belongings, stoned them to death, and burned what remained with fire so that God would represent them once again. Even though God has to deal with us as individuals, it's to bring you to a place where you see yourself as part of the body and not just a body.

When was the last time you saw the pastor put someone out of the church because of disobeying a command of God? The church as we know it would be empty from the pulpit to the doors. So if we choose to just settle for religion and not have God representing us as a people because we refuse to lay aside every weight and sin that so easily besets us, we will never enter the kingdom of God and God will wait on the generation that will. Jesus said it like this in Matthew 18:8–9,

> *If your hand or foot causes you to sin, cut it off and cast it from you. It is better for you to enter into life lame or maimed, rather than having two hands or two feet, to be cast into the everlasting fire. And if your eye causes you to sin, pluck it out and cast it from you. It is better for you to enter into life with one eye, rather than having two eyes, to be cast into hell fire.*

This world and its pleasures, even for a full lifetime of one hundred and twenty years of how you would like to be pleasured, are not worth being cast into everlasting hellfire or continuing to allow those to remain in the church that causes you to sin. The scribes and Pharisees did not teach like this because their lives were full of sin too. You saw them all drop their rocks when they caught the woman in the act of adultery, and all Jesus said was, "You who are without sin, let him cast the first stone." Jesus said they were hindering those who wanted to get into the kingdom because they were not willing to enter themselves, so Jesus said, "I'll do it, and I'll show them the way!" There is no accountability in the body of Christ these days. The church has adopted the ways of the world and its ears to hear what the Spirit is saying. Let's drop down a few verses and see how Jesus tells us to handle offenses.

> *Moreover if your brother sins against you, go and tell him his fault between you and him alone. If he hears you, you have gained your brother. But if he will not hear, take with you one or two more, that "by the mouth of two or three witnesses every word may be established." And if he refuses to hear them, tell it to the church. But if he refuses even to hear the church, let him be to you like a heathen and a tax collector.* (Matthew 18:15–17)

Publicans or tax collectors were well known for their corruption in those days. So Jesus is saying, don't relate to him anymore as a brother but as you would those who are full of corruption. If Jesus came to visit the earth today and got all the news channels to tune in to hear a word He had for His body, I think it would be the first thing He said on His first visit: "Repent, [which means] change the way you think, for the kingdom of heaven is hear!" These words sound so foreign to us because they are from another dimension, and this is how they operate in the heavens—wisdom from above. He told us to pray like this: "Thy kingdom come, Thy will be done, *on earth as it is in heaven!*"

Kingdom surgery

When you think about the church being the actual body of Christ and you look at how it functions on earth from God's perspective, what do you think He thinks? Or if you see the church as His ambassadors representing His kingdom on earth from God's perspective, would or should He be pleased? How about His bride making herself ready for the King and He expects her to look her best for His glory without a spot, blemish, or wrinkle? How does she look? Is she making herself ready? If you see what I see, then you might understand why I titled this book *Enhancing the Kingdom*. The definition of *enhance* is to intensify, increase, or further improve the quality, value, or extent of—all indicating the existence of something that needs work, and in our case, the presence of the kingdom of God on earth today.

Our success is intertwined with each other in the very purpose of God on earth. The King does not take pleasure in those who believe that everything is okay as long as they are doing fine. We are only as strong as our weakest parts. If you were to cut your thumb, your whole body from the head to the toe would come in total agreement to stop the bleeding, clean and treat the wound, bandage it up to keep it clean, and continue with full support from your other hand and fingers, picking up the slack until your thumb was better and ready for duty. That is how God wants to see His church functioning on earth, and He sent His spirit to help us get there.

First Corinthians 12:12–31 (emphasis added) states,

> *For as the body is one and has many members, but*
> *all the members of that one body, being many, are*
> *one body, so also is Christ.*

John says in his writings, "Just as He is, so are we in this world." Then we saw where Paul says, "We are seated with him in heavenly places." So Jesus being one with the church in the world and heavenly places shows how He has joined us to Himself as part of His own body and He being the head making Him one with us.

> *For by one Spirit we were all baptized into one body—*
> *whether Jews or Greeks, whether slaves or free—and*
> *have all been made to drink into one Spirit.*

The Spirit places you in the body and in the territory where you are to function according to the will of the King, not according to your race or gender but the purpose of God.

For in fact the body *is not one member but many.*

Even though His body has many members, it is still only one body, and we need to see ourselves as one with each other in Him.

> *If the foot should say, "Because I am not a hand, I am not of the body," is it therefore not of the body? And if the ear should say, "Because I am not an eye, I am not of the body," is it therefore not of the body? If the whole body were an eye, where would be the hearing? If the whole were hearing, where would be the smelling?*

Think of any of your personal body parts and imagine having to do without them and how you would have to function without that member. That thought places value on each part alone, no matter how insignificant you may have thought before.

> *But now* God has set the members, *each one of them, in the body* just as He pleased. *And if they were all one member, where would the body be?*

Jesus said it was better for them or us that He went because if He did not go, the Holy Ghost would not come, which would mean that God could only be in one place at one time. He also said the works He had done on earth and the greater works we will do because He was going to His Father. He is trying to cover more territory for His glory on the earth, that is what Kings do.

> *But now indeed there are many members, yet one body. And the eye cannot say to the hand, "I have no need of you"; nor again the head to the feet, "I have*

no need of you." No, much rather, those members of the body which seem to be weaker are necessary. And those members of the body which we think to be less honorable, on these we bestow greater honor; and our *unpresentable parts have greater modesty.*

God is saying here, "Do not judge a book by its cover for you do not have a clue what I have deposited in each member to strengthen the body." He has hidden treasures in earthen vessels. Remember, He is the same yesterday, today, and forever. God likes hiding stuff, and just imagine the treasures we would find that would benefit us all if we would heed His word.

But our *presentable parts have no need. But God composed the body, having given greater honor to that part which lacks it, that there should be* no schism *in the body, but that the members should have the same care for one another. And if one member suffers, all the members suffer with it; or if one member is honored, all the members rejoice with it.*

It's easy to rejoice with our member who is honored, but what about when one of our members is wrongfully accused and thrown in jail? Do we not have members who are lawyers and judges and police that God has brought these false accusations to your knowledge? We can't be committed to God and the world.

Now you are the body of Christ, and members individually. And God has appointed these in the church: first apostles, second prophets, third teachers, after that miracles, then gifts of healing, helps, administrations, varieties of tongues. Are all apostles? Are all prophets? Are all teachers? Are all workers of miracles? Do all have gifts of healings? Do all speak with tongues? Do all interpret? But earnestly desire the best gifts. And yet I show you a more excellent way.

You can't be all things to all men within yourself, but we can when we accept our part in the body and the will of Him who placed us here for such a time as this.

Kingdom promotion

I used to be amazed at the fact that when Jesus told His disciples before His ascension to go to Jerusalem and wait until they were endowed with power from on high, there were a hundred and twenty of them waiting with one mind and on one accord. That, in itself, sounded like a miracle to me, with so many people being of the same mind, doing the same thing at the same time, and receiving the Holy Spirit the same way. A hundred and twenty people obeying the command of the Lord and standing in total agreement was quite impressive to me. But now I understand that to God, that was only a seed being planted or a picture of what He expects to grow with the same look and functions as the seed of the hundred and twenty. This command was God about to fulfill what He had promised all throughout the scriptures, the very stone Daniel spoke of being cut out of the mountain without hands in Daniel 2:45. The upper room, also known as the cenacle, is located in the southern part of the old city of Jerusalem *on Mt. Zion*, where they were commanded to wait. The author of Acts 1 is believed to have been Luke but is unknown. The event we are about to look at is where Jesus has already been raised from the dead and is giving His final instructions before His departure from the earth and ascension to the Father. Here, the writer is giving his account of these events to Theophilus, a high priest who was a member of one of the wealthiest and most influential Jewish families in Judaea Province during the first century.

Let's look at Acts 1:1–8, which reads,

> *The former account I made, O Theophilus, of all that Jesus began both to do and teach, until the day in which He was taken up, after He through the Holy Spirit had given commandments to the apostles whom He had chosen, to whom He also*

presented Himself alive after His suffering by many infallible proofs, being seen by them during forty days *and speaking of the things* pertaining to the kingdom of God. *And being assembled together with them,* He commanded *them not to depart from Jerusalem, but to wait for* the promise *of the Father, which, He said, you have heard from Me; for John truly baptized with water, but you shall be baptized with the Holy Spirit* not many days from now. *Therefore, when they had come together, they ask Him, saying, "Lord, will You at this time* restore the kingdom to Israel?" *And He said to them, it is not for you to know times or seasons which the Father has put in His own authority. But you shall receive power when the Holy Spirit has come upon you; and you shall be witnesses to Me in Jerusalem, and in all Judea and Samaria,* and to the end of the earth. (Emphasis added)

In the same way we look back into the garden of Eden and get a picture of God's original intent with man on earth, we can look back on the day of Pentecost and get a picture of God's original intent on the kingdom of God being restored on earth, which in Daniel, he says a kingdom that will not be left to man's rule. All one hundred and twenty obeyed the King's command with one mind and on one accord. The word *kingdom*, in itself, is derived from two words—king and domain. The church is the King's domain. We are the temple of the Holy Spirit, and the kingdom of God is righteousness, peace, and joy in the Holy Ghost. The kingdom is within you, says the King!

Let's look at Paul's letter to the church in Ephesus and see how he addressed the early church in Ephesians 4:1–16 (emphasis added).

I, therefore, the prisoner of the Lord, *I beseech you to* walk worthy *of the calling with which you were called, with all lowliness and gentleness, with long-suffering, bearing with one another* in love, *endeav-*

oring to keep the unity of the Spirit in the bond of peace.

The definition of *endeavor* is to try hard to do or achieve something.

> *There is one body and one Spirit, just as you were called in one hope of your calling; one Lord, one faith, one baptism; one God and Father of all, who is above all, and through all, and in you all. But to each one of us grace was given according to the measure of Christ's gift. Therefore, He says: "When He ascended on high, He led captivity captive, and gave gifts to men."*

Jesus went to hell in our place, and when God raised Him from the dead, Jesus didn't come alone but set the captive free.

> *Now this, "He ascended"—what does it mean but that He also first descended into the lower parts of the earth? He who descended is also the One who ascended far above all the heavens, that He might fill all things. And He Himself gave some to be apostles, some prophets, some evangelists, and some pastors and teachers,* for the equipping *of the saints* for the work *of the ministry, for the edifying of* the body of Christ, till we all come to the unity of the faith and of the knowledge of the Son of God, to a perfect man, *to the measure of the stature* of the fullness of Christ; *that we should no longer be children, tossed to and from and carried about with every wind of doctrine,* by the trickery of men, *in the cunning craftiness of deceitful plotting, but, speaking the truth in love,* may grow up in all things into Him *who is the head—Christ—from whom* the whole body, *joined and knit together by*

> *what every joint supplies,* according to the effective working *by which every part does its share,* causes growth *of the body for the edifying of itself* in love.

Now this word that I'm about to share is for this generation as we all just witnessed God shut the whole planet down with COVID-19 and shift the body around as He sees fit to do what He is about to do on earth and manifest or enhance His kingdom through His body, the church. Verse 13 reveals to us that He wants no more church as usual. He wants the unity of the faith as they were on the day of Pentecost and for the body to understand He is King now and not a president or a prime minister. The buck stops with Him.

> *"All authority has been given to Me in heaven and on earth. Go therefore and* make disciples of all the nations, *baptizing them* in the name *of the Father and of the Son and of the Holy Spirit, teaching them to observe all things that I have* commanded you; *and lo, I am with you always, even to the end of the age."* Amen. (Matthew 28:18–20; emphasis added)

The King is commanding His body to come to order that He may function properly and fill all things, that His work on earth will be effective.

CHAPTER 11

Kingdom Mission

Discipling Nations

WHEN THE LORD said, "Go and make disciples of all the nations," that always seemed to be a very tall order when we could not even make disciples of our cities, communities, or even our homes. If we as individuals are ever going to take the Lord seriously at His command to the church to go and make disciples of all the nations, then for us to obey the command of the King, we must understand that it is impossible for us as individuals to accomplish this mission. No matter how anointed, gifted, and famous you are, it is impossible for you alone to make disciples of all the nations in this world today.

There are one hundred ninety-five countries in the world today, and the King expects the church to go and make disciples of one hundred ninety-five of them. This mandate will not be accomplished on prayer alone, especially if our prayers are to order the King to do what He has commanded us to do. "Dear Lord, save the nations that they may follow you and get to know you for themselves. In Jesus's name, we pray. Amen!" That will not get the job done! God did not position us on earth to be His eyes and notify Him when something is wrong. He places us where He sees fit and allows us to go through and experience the trials and tribulations that will mold us into the characters that He chooses us to be so that we might do His will on earth all the way down to the time and era for you to be on earth.

The parents, teachers, jobs, friends, victories, losses—in other words, all the things that He has allowed you to experience—will work together for good to those who love God and to those who are called according to His purpose. We were predestined to be here at this time to receive this word and to carry out His will on earth for such a time as this. He gave us the fivefold ministry for us to grow up spiritually so that He might reveal to a certain generation that would respond to the King's command and bring glory and honor to His name on earth. The good news is, He has given us the power to accomplish His mandate in the Holy Spirit. "For it is not by might nor by your personal power but by My Spirit," says the Lord! The spirit of the Lord is all-knowing, all-powerful, and already knows how to accomplish the will of Him who sent Him, and if He be for us, who can be against us?

In Paul's letter to the church in Philippi, there are a few verses we need to look at, starting with Philippians 1:27–30 (emphasis added).

> *Only let your conduct be worthy of the gospel of Christ, so that whether I come and see you or am absent, I may hear of your affairs, that you* stand fast in one spirit, *with* one mind *striving together for the faith of the gospel.*

Jesus said, "Every kingdom divided against itself is brought to desolation." The definition of *desolation* is a state of complete emptiness or destruction. If we are going to be effective in our mission, we can no longer walk alone. Only in Christ is real unity and joy possible.

> *And not in any way terrified by your adversaries, which is to them a proof of perdition, but to you of salvation, and that from God.*

God has not given us the spirit of fear but of power, love, and a sound mind. We see all through the scriptures how God's people stood in the face of adversity because of their beliefs and many to their deaths. But this generation just wants the blessings and the opportunity to go to heaven, all on their terms.

> *For to you it has been granted on behalf of Christ,* not only *to believe in Him, but also to suffer for His sake, having the same conflict which you saw in me and now hear is in me.*

Some of us will have to face persecution when we truly obey the Lord because the enemy will not just surrender the territory to us. But the gates of hell will not prevail against us when we make our stand in one spirit, with one mind striving together for the faith of the gospel.

Let's continue into the next chapter of this letter, looking at verses 2:1–11 (emphasis added), which reads,

> *Therefore if there is any consolation in Christ, if any comfort of love, if any fellowship of the Spirit, if any affection and mercy, fulfill my joy* by being like-minded, *having the* same love, *being of* one accord, *of* one mind.

If the church today would change its focus from just you and Jesus to taking your place in Him and submitting to the spirit of God, we can start being effective in our mission on earth and hand the generation after us real hope.

> *Let nothing be done through* selfish ambition or conceit, *but in lowliness of mind let each* esteem others *better than himself. Let each of you look out* not only *for his own interests,* but also *for the interests of others.*

God does not want us self-centered and preoccupied with our own affairs. In Christ, my success is your success, and my failure is your failure, and vice versa. I rejoice when you succeed, and I mourn when you suffer loss because we are all one in Christ.

> *Let* this mind *be in you* which was also *in Christ Jesus, who, being in the form of God, did not consider it robbery to be equal with God, but* made Himself *of no reputation, taking* the form of *a bondservant, and coming in* the likeness *of men. And being found in appearance* as a man, *He* humbled Himself *and* became obedient *to the point of death, even the death of the cross.*

If we are going to be like-minded, have the same love, and be of one accord and one mind like the hundred twenty on the day of Pentecost when God established His kingdom on earth and like Paul is saying in this text, then we all must let this mind be in us as it was in Christ Jesus, who, being God, made Himself of no reputation but was born in a manger and wrapped in swaddling clothes, taking on the form of a man for thirty-three years and dying a horrific death on the cross to obey His Father's will to redeem us. All by His choice, our prime example, we saw verses where it said Jesus was distressed just thinking about what He was going to have to go through to redeem us. And let us not forget Him going to the Father three times, asking Him to take that mission from Him. But nevertheless, "not My will, but Thy will be done!"

Romans 12:1 says, *"I BESEECH you therefore, brethren, by the mercies of God, that* you present *your bodies* a living sacrifice, holy, acceptable to God, *which is* your reasonable service."* We have watered down Christianity long enough. We are to humble ourselves and present our lives to the King to have His way with His property— meaning He owns you too—for it is our reasonable service. We are worthless to the King on earth when we are dead. He's looking for us to become a living sacrifice, meaning we die daily. The alternative is eternity in hell. Remember, Psalm 2:12 says, *"Kiss the Son, lest He be angry, and you perish in the way."*

Remember, the fear of the Lord is the beginning of wisdom. There's been no fear because we haven't been preaching the gospel of the kingdom. His will is *nonnegotiable*. He's no president or prime minister, He's King of kings and Lord of lords!

> *Therefore God also has highly exalted Him and given Him* the name *which is above every name, that at the name of Jesus every knee should bow, of those in heaven, and of those on earth, and of those under the earth, and that every tongue should confess that Jesus Christ is Lord, to the glory of God the Father.*

Servanthood

We saw in the last passage how Christ humbled Himself and stepped down from heaven and His place in the office of being God with the Father and took on the form of a human and a bond servant, which is a person bound in service without wages or a slave or serf. We also see a lot in Paul's letters him referring to himself as a bond servant or slave for Christ because of the things he had to endure for what he was called to do. But the good news is, we are not all called to be the ear, the foot, or the hand. In other words, none of our walks will look the same, and our characteristics will not be the same because we are unique, fearfully and wonderfully made.

Your wilderness experience will be different from mine because of who you are and what He has planned for your life. But we are all necessary and responsible for His mission in one way or another. God places you where He places you according to His good pleasure and whatever He's calling you to do. He has already equipped you with everything you will need to get the job done. There are so many different types of gifts that God has placed in man. He said your gifts will make room for you. They will open doors for you and give you opportunities that others just dream of, and they may even make you rich. God does not have a problem with you being rich here on the earth. In fact, He gets no glory out of you being broke and sick and defeated all the time. They are not broke, sick, and defeated in heaven, and He said to pray that His kingdom come and His will be done on earth just as it is in heaven.

It's His good pleasure to give you the kingdom, but with that type of blessing flowing in your life, there are some things you first must understand. When He tells us that the wealth of the wicked is laid up for the just, it's just like the people of Israel having the promised land filled with giants who are not planning on moving anytime soon. God knows how to transfer His wealth to His children, but we need to understand that in the kingdom, the King owns everything and we own nothing even though he allows us to enjoy it. The gifts and callings of God are irrevocable, which means they cannot be changed, reversed, or recovered. They are final. God has hidden these treasures in earthen vessels called man, and your gift is not for you to make yourself rich, even though it may, but has been entrusted to you to serve it to the body and even the world. When you discover the hidden treasure that He has deposited within you, then you should grow up to the point where you can say, "With my gift, I serve the body of Christ or the world at the pleasure of the King."

Let's look at a few verses in Matthew 20:25–28 that read,

> *But Jesus called them to Himself and said, "You know that the rulers of the Gentiles lord it over them, and those who are great exercise authority over them. Yet it shall not be so among you; but whoever desires to become great among you, let him be your servant. And whoever desires to be first among you, let him be your slave—just as the Son of Man did not come to be served, but to serve, and to give His life a ransom for many."*

We know Jesus was a slave to the will of His Father. One day, they asked Him if He wanted something to eat, and He said, "I have meat to eat that you know not of? My meat is to do the will of Him who sent Me." Paul called himself a slave and a bond servant, which reminds me of those men in Acts 19, where they tried to cast out a devil in the name of Jesus that Paul preached and those devils said, "Jesus—I know, and Paul—I know, but who are you?" Then those devils jumped on those men because they had no greatness working for them in His kingdom. We are all called to serve and to esteem others better than ourselves.

Let's look at a parable in Luke 12:35–48 that reads,

> *Let your waist be girded and your lamps burning; and you yourselves be like men who wait for their master, when he will return from the wedding, that when he comes and knocks they may open to him immediately. Blessed are* those servants *whom the master, when he comes, will find watching. Assuredly, I say to you that he will gird himself and have them sit down to eat, and will come and serve them. And if he should come in the second watch, or come in the third watch, and find them so, blessed are* those servants, *but know this, that if the master of the house had known what hour the thief would come, he would have watched and not allowed his house to be broken into. Therefore you also be ready, for the Son of Man is coming at an hour you do not expect. Then Peter said to Him, "Lord, do You speak this parable only to us,* or to all people?" *And the Lord said, "Who then is that* faithful and wise steward, *whom his master will make ruler over his household, to give them their portion of food in due season? Blessed is* that servant *whom his master will find so doing when he comes. Truly, I say to you that he will make him ruler over all that he has. But if that servant says in his heart, 'My master is delaying his coming,' and begins to beat the male and female servants, and to eat and drink and be drunk, the master of that servant will come on a day when he is not looking for him, and at an hour when he is not aware, and will cut him in two and*

appoint him his portion with the unbelievers. And that servant who knew his master's will, and did not prepare himself or do according to his will, shall be beaten with many stripes. But he who did not know, yet committed things deserving of stripes, shall be beaten with few. For everyone to whom much is given, from him much will be required; and to whom much has been committed, of him they will ask the more. (Emphasis added)

Whether we are still going through our schooling period waiting on our due season or matured and ready to be used by Him for service, we all are to be about His business. The servants who are distracted by the things of the world will receive stripes and their portions with the unbelievers.

The Lord of the Harvest

As of today, the church is responsible for making disciples of one hundred ninety-five nations, and the main thing needed to accomplish such a task is laborers. We have established that this will be a unified effort of believers who are willing to die daily to the flesh and submit their lives to the orders of the Holy Spirit. When God tells us to live our lives as a living sacrifice or for us to be able to follow Him, we must first take up our cross and follow Him lets us know that God does not want us to be focused on ourselves. If you are a self-centered or selfish type of person and you believe that God just wants you to be happy, then it would be impossible for you to join the ranks at this time until you repent or change the way you think. We only get one shot at life; thus, we must obey the King on earth. It is all about Him. There will be no reincarnations or do-overs. It's either "yes, Lord" or "no, Lord" to His will.

James 4:13–17 says,

Come now, you who say, "Today or tomorrow we will go to such and such a city, spend a year there, buy and sell, and make a profit"; whereas you do not know what will happen tomorrow. For what is your life? *It is even a vapor that appears for a little time and then vanishes away. Instead you ought to say,* "If the Lord wills, *we shall live and do this or that. But now you boast in your arrogance.* All such boasting is evil. *Therefore, to him who knows to do good and does not do it, to him it is sin."* (Emphasis added)

We can't have it both ways. Our will and His will being done at the same time would make God a liar because He has already said, "My ways are not your ways." We came into this world with nothing, and we will leave it with nothing. So what does it profit a man to gain the whole world and lose his soul? God wants us to have an abundant life here on earth but not at the expense of His will being ignored. Let's look at the heart of Jesus during His ministry here on earth.

Then Jesus went about all the cities and villages, teaching in their synagogues, preaching the gospel of the kingdom, *and healing every sickness and every disease among the people. But when He saw the multitudes, He was moved with compassion* for them, *because they were weary and scattered, like sheep having no shepherd. Then He said to His disciples,* "The harvest truly is plentiful, but the laborers are few." *Therefore pray the Lord of the harvest to send out laborers into His harvest.* (Matthew 9:35–38; emphasis added)

We can't continue living our lives as if the laborers are meant to be someone else, and we just ask the Lord to send them. Remember Peter's question to the Lord, he asked, "Lord is this parable only to us, or to all people?" It wasn't a hundred ninety-five nations back then, and they still felt overwhelmed. Jesus still has compassion today for the people in the world because they are weary and scattered, like sheep having no shepherd. If the body of Christ chooses not to function under the orders of its head, then how will Psalm 110:1–2 ever be accomplished?

> *The Lord said to my Lord, "Sit at My right hand,*
> *till I make your enemies Your footstool. The Lord*
> *shall send the rod of Your strength* out of Zion. *Rule*
> *in the midst of Your enemies!"* (Emphasis added)

The rod that came out of Zion was a hundred twenty Spirit-filled believers with one mind and of one accord, who were obedient to the King. And if it had not been for their sacrifice, we would still be lost today. How could we even think that we are not responsible for this generation and the generations to come? However many generations it will take for the church to make His enemies a footstool for His feet will be how many it will be because His will and His outcome will remain the same, for it is written.

Let's listen in on Paul's insight on the matter in 1 Corinthians 9:16–23 (emphasis added):

> *For if I preach the gospel, I have nothing to boast of,*
> *for necessity is laid upon me; yes,* woe is me if I do
> not preach the gospel!

Paul is saying that his preaching of the gospel is nothing for him to brag about because he is simply obeying God. It is necessary for him to preach the gospel unless he disobeys the will of God for his life.

> *For if I do this willingly, I have a reward;* but
> if against my will, *I have been entrusted with a*
> *stewardship.*

Paul is saying here that if he obeys the Lord willingly, he will be rewarded, but if he does it against his will, he is still obligated to do the very same thing because it has been entrusted to him to get it done.

> *What is my reward then? That when I preach the gospel, I may present the gospel of Christ without charge, that I may not abuse my authority in the gospel. For though I am free from all men,* I have made myself a servant to all, *that I might win the more; and to the Jews I became* as a Jew, *that I might win Jews; to those who are under the law,* as under the law, *that I might win those who are under the law; to those who are without law,* as without law *[not being without law toward God, but under law toward Christ], that I might win those who are without law; to the weak I became* as weak, *that I might win the weak. I have become all things to all men, that I might by all means save some.*

Paul's strategy was to find ways to relate or identify with all men so that he might save some. He did not go around telling people how they were sinners, what they were doing wrong, and the things they needed to quit doing. That's not what drew you to Christ, but it was His love that drew you. "Now this I do for the gospel's sake, that I may be partaker *of it with you.*" We all have been entrusted with stewardship—the job of supervising or taking care of something such as an organization or property. This is what He meant when He said, "Occupy till I come." We can do it willingly or against our will, but we are still obligated. We will either hear Him say, "Well done, My good and faithful servant" or "Depart from Me, you worker of iniquity, I never knew you."

CHAPTER 12

Kingdom Expectation

Stewardship

PAUL SHOWS US that we have been entrusted with stewardship, and there are two approaches we have in our response to obedience to it—that is willingly or against our will—but the will of the Lord for us concerning it will not change. We are the salt of the earth, not a salt; and we are the light of the world, not a light. God has put the responsibility of the nations getting to know Him and His goodness on the church. And He has placed in every man gifts and treasures that would glorify Him when we choose to walk in obedience to His will.

This has always been the plan of God for man on earth, starting with Adam, whom He made in His image and said, "Be fruitful and multiply; fill the earth and subdue it; have dominion over the fish, birds, and every living thing that moves on the earth." God's plan is—not was—for man to manage His property and to fill it with the glory of God while He rules the seen from the unseen through man. Now since the fall of man, there is a spirit on earth that has blinded the minds of man and corrupted their hearts to where they have become dull of hearing the voice of God; and he is trying to keep as many as he can in captivity to join him in eternal damnation as he roams the land, seeking whom he may devour. But God sent His Son to eradicate sin, redeem man, and restore the original plan for him, which is for him to be fruitful, to multiply, and to fill the earth with the glory of God in Christ Jesus.

Let's hear Paul in 2 Corinthians 4:1–7 (emphasis added):

> *Therefore, since we have this ministry, as we have received mercy,* we do not lose heart. *But we have renounced the hidden things of shame, not walking in craftiness nor handling the word of God deceitfully,* but by manifestation of the truth commending ourselves to every man's conscience in the sight of God. *But even if* our gospel *is veiled, it is veiled to those who are perishing, whose minds the god of this age has blinded, who do not believe,* lest the light *of the gospel of the glory of Christ,* who is the image of God, *should shine on them. For we do not preach ourselves, but Christ Jesus the Lord, and ourselves* your bondservants *for Jesus' sake. For it is God* who commanded light *to shine out of darkness, who has shone in our hearts* to give the light *of the knowledge of the glory of God in the face of Jesus Christ. But* we have this treasure *in earthen vessels,* that the excellence of the power may be of God *and not of us.*

God is commanding once again for light to shine out of darkness, and He has placed that light within His church. He reigns among His enemies, and the gates of hell will not prevail against the church. No weapon that is formed against us will be able to prosper because He always causes us to triumph. We are more than conquerors in Christ Jesus, and the weapons of our warfare are not carnal in no way, shape, or form; but they are mighty through God to the pulling down of strongholds that the enemy has set up over man! Victory for the church is inevitable. We are destined to win, overcome, and have dominion; we are the head and not the tail, above and not beneath.

Jesus said the kingdom of God is like yeast in dough. Once you place yeast in the dough, the whole lump of dough becomes yeast. Let's hear another parable from Jesus as He tells us how we are to manage His property with the treasures He has given us in Luke 19:11–27.

Now as they heard these things, He spoke another parable, because He was near Jerusalem and because they thought the kingdom of God would appear immediately. Therefore, He said: "A certain noble-man went into a far country to receive for himself a kingdom *and to return. So he called ten of his servants, delivered to them ten minas, and said to them, 'Do business till I come.' But his citizens hated him, and sent a delegation after him, saying, 'We will not have this man to reign over us.' And so it was that when he returned,* having received the kingdom, *he then commanded these servants, to whom he had given the money, to be called to him, that he might know how much every man had gained by trading. Then came the first, saying, 'Master, your mina has earned ten minas.' And he said to him, 'Well done, good servant; because you were faithful in a very little,* have authority over ten cities.' *And the second came, saying, 'Master, your mina has earned five minas.' Likewise he said to him, 'You also be over five cities.' Then another came, saying, 'Master, here is your mina, which I have kept put away in a handkerchief.* For I feared you, *because you are an austere man. You collect* what you did not *deposit and reap* what you did not *sow.' And he said to him, 'Out of your own mouth I will judge you, you wicked servant. You knew that I was an austere man, collecting* what I did not *deposit and reaping* what I did not *sow. Why then did you not put my money in the bank, that at my coming I might have collected it with interest?' And he said to those who stood by, 'Take the mina from him, and give it to him who has ten minas.' [But they said to him, 'Master, he has ten minas.'] 'For I say to you, that to everyone who has will be given; and from him who does not have, even what he has will be taken away from him. But bring here those enemies of mine,* who did not want me to reign over them, *and slay them before me.'"* (Emphasis added)

Faithfulness is not a religious word. It is the concept of a steward. The nobleman had entrusted his servants with money or a gift and told them to do business or occupy until he returned from the far country, where he would receive a kingdom. Upon his return, he called the servants whom he had given the stewardship to to see how well they had done one by one. All the servants had been given one mina each, but one had multiplied his by ten and another by five. Then there was one who was walking in fear and not faith and did nothing with his because he felt he was an austere man, which is severe or strict in manner, attitude, or appearance. He also felt he reaped where he did not sow or collected where he personally did not make the deposit. In other words, he chose to believe his feelings above his master and ended up losing what he had as the others were blessed. Let's pray and rise to the call of the Lord sending faithful bond servants into His harvest, for the harvest is plentiful and the labors are few. He rewards the faithful, and for those who do not want Him to reign over them, well, He has something in store for them as well. Remember the Psalms: "Kiss the Son or perish!"

Religious default

In men's pursuit to get to know God for themselves and learn His ways, they have come through some sort of religion. You can spend your entire life and live to be a thousand years old in your pursuit to get to know the great and awesome God that He is, who is also invisible to the naked eye, and still die not fully knowing Him.

Our minds cannot contain the depth of who He is. He is all that you will ever need and so much more after that. But God does want you to diligently seek Him, and it's Him He wants you to seek. We live in a physical dimension, we operate by sight and gather information from what we see in the natural, and we pick up the prayers, rituals, culture, and traditions that religion teaches you in your pursuit of an invisible God. We can't see God, His kingdom, and His angels as they encamp around us. We can't see joy, peace, love, long-suffering, or none of the fruits of the Spirit. We can't see the weapons of our warfare or the war that we are a part of. Therefore, we must walk by faith and not by sight.

To the world, all these things are foolishness to them because the life of faith is spiritually discerned. So how are we to convince the unbeliever that these things are true if we can't even see God working in our own lives to our understanding? Sometimes, the longer you've been involved with religion, the more self-righteous you can become. You can feel because you do this and do that and pray such and such times a day and you don't curse, chew, or hang around those who do and because you are doing the will of God. Then that spirit and attitude goes with you as you try to witness to a lost world, and not only do they feel you are a hypocrite, but we saw how many times Jesus called the scribes and Pharisees who had the same religious spirit. Paul always tried to relate and find common ground as he became like them while among them. Jesus Himself fit in so well with whom He hung around that they had to point Him out when they came to arrest Him. He drank wine while in the company of certain people and, not once, was distracted from His mission. We can be distracted by religion if we're not careful in trying to make it something that it is not. He said our righteousness or our good works are as filthy rags to the Lord! So all the good things that you do and the bad things that you don't do do not mean that you are doing the will of God.

Let's look at Isaiah 58:1–14 (emphasis added), which reads,

> *Cry aloud, spare not; Lift up your voice like a trumpet; Tell My people their transgression, and the house of Jacob their sins.*

God is telling them to go boldly, not hold back, and tell the people what I said and who it is that says it!

> *Yet they* seek Me daily, *and* delight to know *My ways,* as *a nation* that did *righteousness,* and did not *forsake the ordinance of their God.* They ask of Me *the ordinances of justice;* They take delight *in approaching God.*

This verse is basically saying that instead of the people doing the will of God He just commanded in verse one, they are being religious and thinking everything is all good because they are doing good things. A nation that believed they were righteous because of their works only became self-righteous while they were forsaking His ordinances.

> *"Why have* we fasted,*" they say, "and You have not seen? Why have* we afflicted our souls, *and You take no notice?" "In fact, in the day of your fast* you find pleasure, *and exploit* all your laborers. *Indeed* you fast for strife and debate, *and to strike with the fist of wickedness. You will not fast as you do this day,* to make your voice heard on high. Is it a fast that I have chosen, *a day for a man to afflict his soul? Is it to bow down his head like a bulrush, and to spread out sackcloth and ashes?* Would you call this a fast, *and an acceptable day to the Lord?"*

God is not impressed with our rituals, prayers, or traditions if they are not in line with His will. He's not obligated to move on your behalf because you did a spiritual thing with the wrong motives, and He won't. As far as He is concerned, if you were going to disobey Him, you should have eaten while you disobeyed so you didn't have to go hungry instead of trying to replace obedience with a religious act. Now back to verse one, says the Lord (in theory)!

Is this not the fast that I have chosen: *To loose the bonds of wickedness, to undo the heavy burdens, to let the oppressed go free, and that you break every yoke?* Is it not *to share your bread with the hungry, and that you bring to your house the poor who are cast out; When you see the naked, that you cover him, and not hide yourself from your own flesh?* Then your light *shall break forth like the morning,* your healing *shall spring forth speedily, and* your righteousness *shall go before you; The glory of the Lord* shall be *your rear guard.* Then you shall call, *and the Lord will answer;* You shall cry, *and He will say, "Here I am."* If you *take away the yoke from your midst, the pointing of the finger, and speaking wickedness,* If you *extend your soul to the hungry and satisfy the afflicted soul,* then your light *shall dawn in the darkness, and* your darkness shall be as *the noonday. The Lord will* guide you *continually, and* satisfy your soul *in drought, and* strengthen your bones; You shall be like *a watered garden, and like a spring of water, whose waters do not fail. Those from among you shall build the old waste places; You shall raise up the foundations of many generations; And you shall be called the* Repairer of the Breach, The Restorer of Street to dwell in. *If you turn away your foot from the Sabbath, from* doing your pleasures *on My holy day, and call the Sabbath a delight, the holy day of the Lord honorable, and shall honor Him,* not doing your own ways, *nor finding* your own pleasure, *nor speaking* your own words, Then you shall *delight yourself in the Lord; And* I will *cause you to ride on the high hills* of the earth, *and feed you with the heritage of Jacob your father.* The mouth of the lord has spoken.

God is saying in this chapter, "I see you playing church and liking the goose bumps and the good messages, and you even got the rituals down, but you wonder why you haven't seen all the blessings I promised to you manifested in your lives? It is because what you have settled for is not who you are and is not what I have called you to be on earth." If we get on the same page and get in one accord with the same mindset that Jesus demonstrated to us and answer the call of the Lord, then this world would not see us as foolish people anymore but as peculiar people, whom God has so blessed that it provokes them to jealousy, where our lives will be the witness of God and they come to us asking what must they do to be saved. We are not waiting on God, He has been waiting on us. And He has all eternity to wait on the generation that will respond to His will for us. Second Chronicles 7:14 states, *If My people who are called by My name humble themselves and pray and seek My face and turn from their wicked ways, then I will hear from heaven and forgive their sin and heal their land.* Therefore, when He said quit the finger-pointing, it means no more blaming the government, other races, other religions, other nations, or whatever helps you sleep at night. Let's together take the responsibility that He has given to the church and enhance the kingdom of God as we take our place of walking in dominion and be ambassadors that bring glory and honor to His name.

Repairers of the Breach

There is a breach that is in need of repair, and the church is the only one who has been authorized by the King to repair it. What is a breach? The definition of *breach* is an act of breaking or failing to observe a law, agreement, or code of conduct. God is saying, "If you ignore my will, I will ignore your will." We can't change what we won't acknowledge, but we can change what we do. The church has failed to observe His laws as we have greased ourselves down with His grace as an alternative and the church's code of conduct, which is a set of values, rules, standards, and principles, outlining what the King expects from His church within His kingdom.

We know that changes every time you visit a different ministry because of how divided we allowed the enemy to keep us. Instead of us having one mind, we have millions. And instead of being in one accord, we're blessed when we can find one or two to agree with us. Everyone won't answer this call at once. But for those who have an ear to hear what the Spirit is saying to the church, I have good news for you: God is no respecter of persons. Acts 10:34–35 states, "*Then Peter opened his mouth and said: 'In truth I perceive that God shows no partiality. But in every nation whoever fears Him and works righteousness is accepted by Him.'*" Therefore, when we lay aside every sin and weight that so easily besets us, we start seeing ourselves as one in Christ Jesus as God sees us.

Galatians 3:16 says, "*Now to Abraham and his Seed were the promises made. He does not say, 'And to seeds,' as of many, but as of one, 'And to your Seed,' who is Christ.*" We have been seated with Him in heavenly places, and we are joint heirs with Him. So when God says, "I wish above all things that you prosper and be in health even as your soul prospers," the wealth of the wicked is laid up for the just. This breach that we have caused has been the problem all along in making these promises become our reality. If we choose to observe His laws and His commandments, then there is healing for everybody in His kingdom. For by His stripes, we were healed. And everybody will be rich because, in a kingdom, it is the King's responsibility to take care of His citizens. There will be a commonwealth where all your needs are met according to His riches in glory. He became poor so that you might be rich. Everybody's light is shining, and everybody's darkness will be as the noonday. Everybody's soul will be satisfied, and we will all be like a watered garden. And when we call on Him, he will answer us. This is why the generations that come after the generation that responds to the will of the Lord will call them the Repairers of the Breach and the Restorer of Streets to dwell in. Our world is getting worse like religion teaches us to declare it. And the church is in a standoff with the King—a standoff that we have no chance of winning but can choose to continue to ignore His will and just die in the wilderness as God waits on that Joshua generation who says enough is enough.

I believe God is saying this to this generation right now, and He will wait for our response to His invitation. For it is His good pleasure to give us the kingdom, He has all the time in the world, literally! I believe that God will make a spectacle of those who respond to His will and those who ignore it within the body because He is ready to show Himself mighty, to throw His weight around!

Let's hear the words of the King in Matthew 25:31–46 (emphasis added):

> *When the Son of Man comes in His glory, and all the holy angels with Him, then He will sit on the throne of His glory. All the nations will be gathered before Him, and He will separate them one from another, as a shepherd divides his sheep from the goats. And He will set the sheep on His right hand, but the goats on the left. Then the King will say to those on His right hand, "Come, you blessed of My Father, inherit the kingdom prepared for you from the foundation of the world: for I was hungry and you gave Me food; I was thirsty and you gave Me drink; I was a stranger and you took Me in; I was naked and you clothed Me; I was sick and you visited Me; I was in prison and you came to Me." Then the righteous will answer Him, saying, "Lord, when did we see you hungry and feed You, or thirsty and give You drink? When did we see You a stranger and take You in, or naked and clothe You? Or when did we see You sick, or in prison, and come to You?" And the King will answer and say to them, "Assuredly, I say to you, inasmuch as you did it to one of the least of these My brethren, you did it to Me." Then He will also say to those on the left hand, "Depart from Me, you cursed, into the everlasting fire prepared for the devil and his angels: for I was hungry and you gave Me no food; I was thirsty and you gave Me no drink; I was a stranger and you did*

not take Me in, naked and you did not clothe Me, sick and in prison and you did not visit Me." Then they also will answer Him, saying, "Lord, when did we see you hungry or thirsty or a stranger or naked or sick or in prison, and did not minister to You?" Then He will answer them, saying, Assuredly, I say to you, in as much as you did not do it to one of the least of these, you did not do it to Me. And these will go away into everlasting punishment, *but the righteous* into eternal life.

Oh, when the saints go marching in; Oh, when the saints go marching in; Oh, how I want to be in that number when the saints go marching in! Our lives are but a vapor. We are here today and gone tomorrow. I don't know about you, but I don't want to get to the final judgment, and when the King starts dividing the sheep from the goats, I find myself in the goat line because some other goat told me it was all good while I was in the land of the living. I choose to join my brothers and sisters in submitting my life to the will of the King and be a repairer of the breach. In Jesus's name, amen!

Kingdom Influence

One with the Trinity

TO MAKE SURE that we don't end up in the goat line on the day of judgment, we need to understand how we are to do what He is calling us to do. We need to know how we are to relate to the invisible King in a visible world, establishing an invisible kingdom, which we are governed by as we live in this visible world that we are not of anymore. And because the world does not operate on heaven's frequency, the way you live your life on earth should not only be viewed by the world as peculiar but also foolish in some cases. But why should we care what man thinks about us if we are living our lives as living sacrifices? In other words, as we take up our crosses daily, we become dead to ourselves but alive to God—dead to what's natural and alive to that which is supernatural or spiritual. Our citizenship is in heaven, and we live our lives for now on earth, representing to the world our home country. In our home country, there are three that bear records in the heavens, and the three are one. Each one of them with their own unique personality, which is the combination of characteristics or qualities that form an individual's distinctive character. And these three are one, which is to say, they are with one mind and with one accord.

Now we, too, have been adopted into the family of God. Our heavenly Father wants us to be about the family's business and has made us one with Him in Christ Jesus and wants us to be of the same mind and with the same accord. God created us in His own image and likeness and expects us to grow up into the new man that we are in Him and carry out His plans and purposes on earth in His Son's name by His spirit. Jesus, in His ministry on earth, demonstrated to us how we are to relate to the King in how He related to His Father like an ambassador. I know we covered that He only said what His Father said and only did what His Father said to do. And even in the garden of Gethsemane, where He prayed earnestly to the Father that if it is so, to take that bitter cup from Him lest He drinks it and concluded with, "Not My will but Thy will be done."

I also want us to think about Jesus at twelve years old as Joseph and Mary took Him and the family to observe the Passover as was their custom. The Bible says the boy Jesus lingered behind in Jerusalem. In other words, Jesus ditched His earthly parents to do His heavenly Father's business. Only twelve at the time and in Jewish custom, you had to be thirty for them to consider you to be a real rabbi or teacher. But still, He knew who He was and why He was on earth at twelve. Or how about the story when Jesus's mother and brothers came to where He was speaking and stood outside, desiring to speak with Him? He told the one who told Him, "Who is My mother, and who are My brothers?" He then told them, "For whoever does the will of My Father in heaven is My brother and sister and mother."

The will of His Father and His heavenly family superseded His earthly relationships, and He expects the same from us. He told this man to follow Him, and his response was that he would, but first, let him go and bury his father. And Jesus replied, "Let the dead bury their own dead, but you go and preach the kingdom of God." Then another man said, "Lord, I will follow you, but let me first go a bid them farewell who are at my house." But Jesus said to him, "No one, having put his hand to the plow and looking back, is fit for the kingdom of God." When God tells us to seek first the kingdom, He means to seek first! This is a King talking to us, and we do not comprehend royal etiquette. God knows who He is, and He knows that there is no one greater than Himself. If He declares Himself to be King, then it is settled since there is no one or nothing that can tell Him He's not! If He wanted us to relate to Him and assume that all is well and wanted us to believe that our opinions matter, He would take them into consideration. He would not have referred to Himself as a King. He could have left it as a loving Father, which He is for certain seasons of our lives, but He is also the King.

Let's look at John's letter starting in John 14:22–26 (emphasis added):

> *Judas [not Iscariot] said to Him, "Lord, how is it that You will manifest Yourself to us, and not to the world?" Jesus answered and said to him, "If anyone loves Me,* he will keep My words; *and My Father will love him, and We will come to him and make Our home with him. He who does not love Me* does not keep My words; *and the word which you hear is not Mines but the Father's who sent Me. These things I have spoken to you while being present with you. But the Helper, the Holy Spirit, whom the Father will send in My name, He will teach you all things, and bring to your remembrance all things that I said to you."*

God does not expect you to do what He has commanded alone, nor does He expect us to do it by working together without help. He has placed us all where He sees fit and has joined us to Him so that we all be one in Him with the same mind and in one accord, accomplishing His plans and purposes on earth.

Now let's drop down to chapter 15:1–11 (emphasis added):

> *I Am the true vine, and My Father is the vinedresser. Every branch* in Me *that does not bear fruit He takes away; and every branch that bears fruit He prunes, that it may bear more fruit. You are already clean because of the word which I have spoken to*

you. Abide in Me, *and* I in you. *As the branch cannot bear fruit* of itself, *unless it abides in the vine, neither can you, unless you abide in Me. I am the vine, you are the branches. He who abides* in Me, *and* I in him, *bears much fruit; for* without Me *you can do nothing. If anyone does not abide in Me,* he is cast out *as a branch and is withered; and they gather them and throw them into the fire, and they are burned. If you abide in Me, and My words abide in you, you will ask* what you desire, *and* it shall be done for you. *By this My Father is glorified, that you bear much fruit; so you will be My disciples. As the Father loved Me, I also have loved you;* abide in My love. If *you keep My commandments,* you will *abide in My love, just as I have kept My Father's commandments and abide in His love. These things I have spoken to you, that* My joy *may remain in you, and that* your joy *may be full.*

The only way that we abide in the vine and abide in His love and bear much fruit and not be cast out as a branch and wither just to be burned is to keep His commandments. When we keep His commandments, God is pleased, and then we can ask what we desire, and it will be done for us. God wants you to be blessed on earth that He might put your life on display and provoke the world to jealousy, and He is glorified. Abundant life is our reality!

Agape Love

When we hear the word *love,* the meaning we have of that word is based on our past experiences with those who said they loved us or were supposed to have loved us. Therefore, none of our definitions would be the same. Even our personal experiences with God's love toward us as individuals will have us questioning what love is based on things we went through in our lives and didn't understand at the time. No matter what our past experiences with the word love are, whether it was good or bad, we have never given up on the idea of it because God has created man to long for it or to have the need to live by it. Jesus told us we need to abide in His love, and the way that we do that is to keep His commandments. His love will absolutely be different from whatever definition we have come up with based on our past experiences because He knows exactly what love is. God is love, and the only way that we can demonstrate the love required in the kingdom of God is to abide in His love.

Jesus was asked a question we should look at in Matthew 22:36–40:

> *Teacher, which is the great commandment in the law? Jesus said to him, "You shall love the Lord your God with all your heart, with all your soul, and with all your mind.") This is the first and great commandment. And the second is like it: "You shall love your neighbor as yourself." On these two commandments hang all the Law and the Prophets.*

Jesus has just simplified in that very statement what the destination of the work that He has begun in you is, what His finished work in you will look like. He sums up everything that you've been through and still have ahead of you and will all work together to bring you to the place where you choose to walk fully by these two commandments. He said, "If you love Me, you will keep My commandment. If you do not keep My commandments, it is them who do not love Me." His love is always demonstrated with actions and not just lip service. What if God, knowing the state of man after the fall that they were all bound to spend eternity in hell separated from Him, opened up the skies while shaking His head and said, "I so love you," and then closed the skies and watched us all go to hell one by one? Him telling us how He so loved us would have done us no good at all. He didn't just tell us, but He showed us by giving His only begotten Son to die in our place. And Jesus showed us by becoming sin and laying down His life for us. He said, "No man has the power to take My life, but I lay it down," even knowing all He would have to go through to get it done. That's what Jesus means when He says, "If you keep My commandments," because love is action, not feelings. No actions, no love!

So what I want you to see is why Jesus ties these two commandments together. If you do the great one first, which is to love God with all your heart, soul, and mind, then you will do what He wants you to do in the second, which is to love your neighbor as yourself. But you can't do the second without doing the first because, without Him, you can do nothing. He is love, so it would be impossible to love someone without love. That's what I mean we were created to need it and live by it. When we were looking at Paul's writings in 1 Corinthians 12, teaching us about the body being a many-membered man and how God has placed gifts in the body, he ended in that chapter by saying, "And yet I show you a more excellent way."

Well, let's look at that way in 1 Corinthians 13:1–13 (emphasis added):

> *Though I speak with the tongues of men and of angels,* but have not love, *I have become sounding brass or a clanging cymbal. And though I have the gift of prophecy, and understanding all mysteries and all knowledge, and though I have all faith, so that I can remove mountains,* but have not love, *I am nothing. And though I bestow all my goods to feed the poor, and though I give my body to be burned,* but have not love, *it profits me nothing. Love suffers long and is kind; love does not envy; love does not parade itself, is not puffed up; does not behave rudely, does not seek its own, is not provoked, thinks no evil; does not rejoice in iniquity, but rejoices in the truth; bears all things, believes all things, hopes all things, endures all things.* Love never fails. *But whether there are prophecies, they will fail; whether there are tongues, they will cease; whether there is knowledge, it will vanish away. For we know in part and we prophesy in part. But when that which is*

perfect has come, then that which is in part will be done away. When I was a child, I spoke as a child, I understood as a child, I thought as a child; but when I became a man, I put away childish things. For now we see in a mirror, dimly, but then face to face. Now I know in part, but then I shall know just as I also am known. And now abide faith, hope, love, *these three;* but the greatest of these is love.

Paul says the greatest of the three is love and tells us that without love, you are making a lot of noise, but it is not effective and profits you nothing. We are to be driven by the love of God. When you wake up in the morning, He should be the first thing on your mind, and you can't wait to get out of bed to go and show Him how much you love Him by doing the things that please Him. We should be so enjoying an intimate relationship with Him that if we never got the Cadilac or the big house with the big bank account, as long as we are able to wake up to Him, we don't need anything else. God said to Solomon, "Ask what I shall give you?" God had just given Solomon a blank check. You don't need any genie in a bottle that will grant you three wishes when God gives you a blank check. First King 3:6–14 is Solomon's response to God's unbelievable offer. But I want to point out that verse 3 says that Solomon loved the Lord and walked in the statutes of his father, David. So in verse 6, he began to fill in the blank check.

And Solomon said: "You have shown great mercy to Your servant David my father, because *he walked before You in truth, in righteousness, and in uprightness of heart with You; You have continued this great kindness for him, and You have given him a son to sit on his throne, as it is this day." Now, O Lord my God, You have made Your servant king instead of my father David, but I am a little child; I do not know how to go out or come in. And* Your servant *is in the midst of* Your people *whom*

You have chosen, *a great people, too numerous to be numbered or counted. Therefore, give to* Your Servant *an understanding heart to judge* Your people, *that I may discern between good and evil. For who is able to judge this great people* of Yours? The speech pleased the Lord, *that Solomon had asked this thing. Then God said to him:* "Because you have asked this thing, and have not asked long life for yourself, *nor have asked riches* for yourself, *nor have asked the life* of your enemies, *but have asked for yourself understanding to discern justice, behold, I have done according to your words; see, I have given you a wise and understanding heart, so that there has not been anyone like you before you, nor shall any like you arise after you.* And I have also given you *what you have not asked:* both riches and honor, *so that there shall not be anyone like you among the kings all your days. So* if you walk *in My ways, to keep My statutes and My commandments, as your father David walked,* then I will *lengthen your days.*" (Emphasis added)

All Solomon wanted from God was the ability to be a better servant to God as he was now the one to represent His people. Then God said, "Since you have made your request all about Me and My will with My people, I also have given you what you did not ask for." Then Solomon became the richest and wisest king that ever lived. Solomon was raised to love and obey God by a father who was constantly after God's heart and found himself to be like a little child at his appointed time. You will not inherit your parent's discipline and obedience toward God but must serve Him for yourself.

Promotion to friends

Through all the training that God takes you through with your personal trials and tribulations to allow your spirit man to grow up and become who He has called you to be, there is a day of graduation from certain levels. Not saying that you will arrive at a place of no opposition, but as Moses told the people of Israel, "The enemies you see today, you will see them no more!" God does not want you to settle for anything short of what He has promised to His children. But just like a good parent does not hand over their fortunes to an immature child lest he ends up like the prodigal son who wastes his inheritance on riotous living from a lack of knowledge, bringing himself down to the hog's pin, eating slop with the pigs. Once you become born again, it's your spirit man that is the infant and the spiritual man that God relates to. He begins to feed His child the elementary things of the gospel, which He calls the sincere milk of the word.

> *Therefore, laying aside all malice, all deceit, hypocrisy, envy, and all evil speaking,* as new born babes, *desire the pure milk of the word,* that you may grow thereby, *if indeed you have tasted that the Lord is gracious.* (1 Peter 2:1–3; emphasis added)

As your spirit man begins to grow, your feeding on the word will become meat to your spirit man, for the word of God will always be your spiritual food. Jesus said, "Man shall not live by bread alone, but by every word that proceeded out of the mouth of God." Your natural man needs the bread, but your spirit man needs the word of God. If we were to liken our spiritual journey to going through school, we know that there will be assignments given to us that are followed up with tests to see the knowledge that we have contained and the faith that we have in the word that we have received.

The enemy comes in during the test to cause you to lose focus on what your heavenly Father is doing in your life and pulls your focus to the natural realm, and if we choose to believe what we see in the natural over what God is doing in the spiritual realm, we will flunk the test, and God will have you take it again with a different circumstance. We can stay in the second grade for our whole lives in the spirit if we choose to continue to walk by sight and not by faith, prolonging our maturity in the spirit because of idolatry. Paul said when he was a child, he spoke as a child, he thought as a child, but as he became a man, he put childish things away. God has made you a joint heir with Jesus, and if He was to release the level of blessing that He is withholding for you too early, it would destroy you and you would end up in the hogs pin sharing slop with the pigs. Remember Galatians 4:1–2. It says, *"Now I say that the heir, as long as he is a child, does not differ at all from a slave, though he is master of all, but is under guardians and stewards until the time appointed by the Father."* I believe God is saying to the church today, "This is the appointed time for me to release to you your inheritance."

As we begin to repair the breach and obey His commands and walk in His statutes, which is a written law passed by a legislative body in its definition, we will inherit the kingdom, which contains everything our heart desires. First Corinthians 2:9 says, *"But as it is written: 'Eye has not seen, nor ear heard, nor have entered into the heart of man the things which God has prepared for those who love Him.'"* In our growth in the spirit, there will be a graduation or a promotion from servants to friends when we get to the place where we are of the same mind and in one accord with the King.

Let's pick up where we left off in John 15:12–27 (emphasis added):

> *This is My commandment, that you love one another* as I have loved you. *Greater love has no one than this, than to lay down one's life for his friends. You are My friends* if you do *whatever I command you.* No longer do I call you servants, *for a servant does not know what his master is doing;* but I have called you friends, *for all things that I heard from My Father I have made known to you. You did not choose Me, but I chose you and appointed you* that you should go and bear fruit, *and that your fruit should remain, that* whatever you ask *the Father in My name He may give you. These things I command you, that you love one another.*

Now as you go forth to be the generation that repairs the breach, know this:

> *If the world hates you, you know that it hated Me before it hated you. If you were of the world, the world would love its own. Yet because you are not of the world, but I chose you out of the world, therefore the world hates you. Remember the word that I said to you, "A servant is no greater than his master." If they persecuted Me, they will also persecute you. If they kept My word, they will keep yours also. But all these things they will do to you for My name's sake, because they do not know Him who sent Me. If I had not come and spoken to them, they would have no sin,* but now *they have no excuse for their sin. He who hates Me hates My Father also. If I had not done among them the works which no one else did, they would have no sin; but now they have seen and also hated both Me and My Father. But this happened that the word might be fulfilled which is written in their law, "They hated Me without a cause." But when the Helper comes, whom I shall send to you from the Father, the Spirit of truth who proceeds from the Father, He will testify of Me. And you also will bear witness, because you have been with Me from the beginning.*

We, the people of God who used to be destroyed from a lack of knowledge, have now obtained knowledge by the spirit of God and abiding in the vine. He no longer calls us servants but now calls us friends because we have become one with Him, with the same mind and on one accord. "By this shall all men know that you are My disciples, if you have love one for another" (John 13:35). That's the lifestyle of the kingdom of God—on earth as it is in heaven!

CHAPTER 14

Kingdom Motives

Friend or Foe

WHEN JESUS SAID He no longer calls us servants but He now calls us friends, we need to try to comprehend what a friend of God looks like. There is a big difference in the way you would relate to a servant than to a friend. A servant is expected to do what his master commands him to do simply because he was told to do it, but with a friend, it is a shared experience with an agreement nature to it as they do the deed as one. A true friend of God would have to have his belief system in line with the will of God, not only for his life but also His will and plans for the whole church. A true friend of God would have to be able to discern the true nature of the spirit as they fellowship with their heavenly Father because He is a spirit and those who worship Him must worship Him in spirit and truth.

He is holy and pure in His very essence, and we commonly approach our heavenly Father with our carnal minds instead of the mind of Christ and our carnal ways instead of His ways and attempt to relate to a God who is spirit through our flesh. A true friend of God would understand that the carnal mind is enmity against God, and there is no way to please Him in our flesh. That's why He says that without faith, it is impossible to please Him because you have to abide in His realm to relate to Him.

For those who live according to the flesh set their minds *on the things of the flesh, but those who live according to the Spirit, the things of the Spirit. For to be* carnally minded *is death, but to be* spiritually minded *is life and peace. Because the carnal mind is enmity against God; for it is not subject to the law of God, nor indeed can be. So then,* those who are in the flesh cannot please God. *But you are not in the flesh but in the Spirit, if indeed the Spirit of God dwells in you. Now if anyone does not have the Spirit of Christ, he is not His. And if Christ is in you, the body is dead because of sin, but the Spirit is life because of righteousness.* (Romans 8:5–10; emphasis added)

Why do we assume that it doesn't matter how we relate to God when He is clearly saying here that the carnal mindset is enmity against God, which is the state or feeling of being actively opposed or hostile to someone or something. God does not see those who walk according to the flesh as friends when they are actively opposed or hostile toward Him and His purpose on earth. This would be the very reason why you would see Jesus call Judas Iscariot's friend and call Peter the devil. It was Judas who betrayed Jesus by giving Him into the Romans' hands to eventually be crucified, and it was Peter who preached the inaugural address of the church on the day of Pentecost. He called Judas friend at the very moment he was getting ready to betray Him and called Peter the devil when he tried to detour Jesus from having to go to the cross and die for our sins. These are the ways that would not make sense to the carnal mind. So we can understand why Jesus called Judas friend because the very thing he was about to go and do was the very will of God for the life of Jesus. Peter trying to rebuke Jesus for telling them about His death was actively opposed or hostile toward the purpose of God for Jesus.

When Adam fell into the garden, we heard God ask the question, "Adam, where are you?" He had died in the spirit and, therefore, left the very realm in which he had related to God. God has not changed, and if we choose not to change by crucifying our flesh daily and living our lives as a living sacrifice, then we will not have fellowship with our heavenly Father nor be able to please Him as we make ourselves the enemy of God. Religion has taught us religious ways to try to relate to God and to communicate with Him through our prayers as we abide in our flesh. We continue to practice these methods we've learned even when we know that our fellowship with Him is lacking and our prayers are not being answered. There are all kinds of different practices because there are all kinds of different religions. God wants us to learn to discern the realm in which we operate so that He might have more friends working with Him than all of those who work against Him.

Let's look at James 4:1–10 (emphasis added):

> *Where do wars and fights come from among you? Do they not come from your desires for pleasure that war in your members? You lust and do not have. You murder and covet and cannot obtain. You fight and war. Yet you do not have because you do not ask. You ask and do not receive, because you ask amiss, that you may spend it on your pleasures.* Adulterers and adulteresses! *Do you not know that friendship with the world is enmity with God? Whoever therefore wants to be a friend of the world* makes himself an enemy of God. *Or do you think that the Scripture says in vain, "The Spirit who dwells in us yearns jealously?" But He gives more grace. Therefore, He says: "God resists the proud, but gives grace to the humble." Therefore* submit to God. Resist the devil *and he will flee from you.* Draw near to God *and He will draw near to you.* Cleanse your hands, *you sinners; and* purify your hearts, *you double-minded. Lament and mourn and weep! Let your laughter be turned to mourning and your joy to gloom.* Humble yourselves *in the sight of the Lord, and He will lift you up.*

We can hear in the question when He asked, "Where do wars and fights come from among you?" that God Himself does not identify with the cravings of our flesh and pities us as we make ourselves His enemy with the choices we make to satisfy our natural pleasures. His being pure and holy in His essence causes Him not to be able to relate to the sinful nature that is in our flesh.

> *Seeing then that we have a great High Priest who has passed through the heavens,* Jesus the Son of God, *let us hold fast our confession. For we do not have a High Priest who cannot sympathize with our weaknesses, but was in all points* tempted as we are, *yet without sin. Let us therefore come boldly to the throne of grace, that we may obtain mercy and find grace to help in time of need.* (Hebrews 4:14–16; emphasis added)

Let's look at our prayer life and see where our prayers are rooted and determine ourselves if we've been asking amiss and if we have chosen to be friends with the world instead of God. Let's take a good look at our own motives in the things we do and pray to try to understand our own behaviors by asking ourselves why we do the things we do or ask for what we are asking for. A *motive* is a reason for doing something, especially one that is hidden or not obvious. But we also have a high priest who sympathizes with our weaknesses, and His grace is sufficient for us.

Effectual Prayer

When we make our attempts to let our petitions be made known to God and then go on to see that our prayers are not being answered, why do we continue to pray the same way as always and somehow expect to receive a different result? They say that very act is the basic definition of insanity—the state of being seriously mentally ill, madness. The majority of us continue to believe in the power of prayer even when our personal prayer life is unfruitful. We know that the God we are attempting to cast our care upon is real and has made a way for us to let our petitions be made known unto Him. God wishes above all things that you would prosper and be in health even as your soul prospers, and you wish above all things the very same things.

There is something that we are missing in our approach to prayer, and we should look at some things to see if we can find where we are missing it. First, when we come to God, we must believe that He is and that He is a rewarder of those who diligently seek Him. Then we must have the faith without doubt in our hearts that the petitions that we are bringing before Him line up with His will and He can do what He has promised. Jesus during His earthly ministry always made the time to separate Himself from His disciples and go and pray to His Father. But when He was about to raise Lazarus from the dead, He thanked His Father for hearing His prayer and then said, "I know that You always hear Me when I pray." Why is it that the Father would always hear Jesus when He prays, and with us now being the righteousness of God in Christ Jesus, and made to be one with Him, a joint heir with Him, that our prayers sometimes fall by the wayside? Let's keep Jesus in mind as we explore to find out where we might be missing it.

> *Now this is the confidence that we have in Him, that if we ask anything* according to His will, *He hears us. And if we know that He hears us, whatever we ask, we know that we have the petitions that we have asked of Him.* (1 John 5:14–15; emphasis added)

One of the things we see is that the Lord always prayed in line with the will of the Father, with the exception of His petitions in the garden of Gethsemane, when He asked, "If it be so, that He would take that bitter cup from Him lest He drink it?" And He finished the prayer with, "Nevertheless, not My will, but Your will be done." So any prayer that does not line up with His will, He does not hear. For example, God will not bless you to rob a bank or give you someone else's spouse for your own or any other thing that is obviously not His will. Then you must discern where the reason for your prayer originates from. Is it from my flesh? Something to be desired to spend upon my pleasures. Or is it from my spirit? Something that will cause me to grow and become who He's calling me to be. Remember, Solomon asked for wisdom that he might serve the Lord better in his calling, and God gave him what he did not ask for—riches and long life. Now with us still keeping Jesus in mind, this one may be where a lot of us stumble in our attempts at prayer, and that is Mark 11:25–26.

> *And whenever you stand praying, if you have anything against anyone, forgive him, that your Father in heaven may also forgive you your trespasses. But if you do not forgive, neither will your Father in heaven forgive your trespasses.*

You know the story when the men brought the paralytic lying on the bed to Jesus and Jesus tells the paralytic, "Be of good cheer; your sins are forgiven you," placing the man in right standing with the heavenly Father in order to receive from Him, and then told Him to take up his bed and go home. When we allow our contentions to go unchecked and go on as if we do not have discord with our brother and just enter His gates with thanksgiving in our hearts and His courts with praise and His throne with unforgiveness in our hearts, He can't forgive you because you have not forgiven someone, which causes your prayer to be null and void.

> *Therefore, if you bring your gift to the altar, and there remember that your brother has something against you, leave your gift there before the altar, and go your way. First be reconciled to your brother, and then come and offer your gift.* (Matthew 5:23–24)

For Jesus to tell us to first be reconciled to our brother before offering up our gifts or petitions unto the Father lets us know that when we don't reconcile first, our prayers will be hindered. Right standing with Him indicates that there is a way to be in the wrong standings with Him in our prayers. We see how God tells the husband to dwell with his wife with understanding, giving honor to the wife as to the weaker vessel and as being heirs together of the grace of life, so that your prayers may not be hindered. So we plainly see how our prayers to our heavenly Father can be hindered in the way we relate to others or in our refusal to forgive and make peace with one another. If we looked at prayer as a tool that was given to us from our heavenly Father in order to let our request be made known unto Him, then, like any other tool, we would have to follow the instructions that come with it to get the best results as we learn to use it properly.

Now with us understanding that our prayers can be hindered because of the way we relate to others, let us begin to practice. James 5:16 states, *"Confess your trespasses to one another, and pray for one another, that you may be healed. The effective, fervent prayer of a righteous man avails much."* To be righteous is simply to be in the right standing with the Father, and we will not be in the right standing with Him if we refuse to be reconciled to our brothers whom we can see.

> *We love Him because He first loved us. If someone says, "I love God," and hates His brother, he is a liar; for he who does not love his brother whom he has seen, how can he love God whom he has not seen? And this commandment we have from Him: that he who loves God must love his brother also. (1 John 4:19–21)*

We have to clean out our prayer pipes by treating those we see with honor, respect, love, and forgiveness.

Kingdom Prayer

Now let's look at prayer from God's perspective. We have close to eight billion people on the planet today, with most of them having gone to God in some type of prayer for something at some time in some way. And while we all come in so many different ways to Him in prayer, He is busy watching over His word to perform it and looking at your covenant's standing with Him, your heart's motive about your request, and your faith and confession pertaining to the petition. Now in our early walk with Him, any type of approach would do; but as we begin to mature, there are some things that God wants us to understand about the tool of prayer. For instance, when we come to God with our petitions as mature saints, we should know who it is that we are approaching with the petitions. He's not Santa Claus or some genie from a bottle that's here to grant your every wish and command and do the things that sound so spiritual in our prayers as He has told us to do, such as feed the hungry, clothe the naked, or disciple nations. He's not a president or prime minister who is there to take into account your opinions and perspectives on matters and how you think things should unfold. He's King, and beside Him, there is no other! God's preference on the matter is that man ought to always pray and not faint or lose heart when our fiery trials and tribulations come our way to test our faith. We must walk with the knowledge that this thing will surely come to pass and we're not in this by ourselves. It is not living our lives with no communion with Him, and then when something goes wrong, we want to bust into His throne room all frantic with our concerns and just say whatever comes to mind without entering His gates with thanksgiving in our hearts, into His courts with praise, and into His presence with a spirit of worship and gratitude with reverence of our majesty on high.

> *Be anxious for nothing, but in everything by prayer and supplication, with thanksgiving, let your request be made known to God. And the peace of God, which surpasses all understanding will guard your hearts and minds through Christ Jesus.* (Philippians 4:6–7)

To be anxious is to experience worry, unease, or nervousness, typically about an imminent event or something with an uncertain outcome. God said to be anxious for nothing, but with thanksgiving in your hearts, let your requests be made known. God is not interested in watching His children who were created in His image panic or be anxious for nothing, nor is He interested when we come to Him in our own self-righteousness and with our religious-type prayers.

> *And when you pray, you should not be like the hypocrites. For they love to pray standing in the synagogues and on the corners of the streets, that they may be seen by men. Assuredly, I say to you, they have their reward. But you, when you pray, go into your room, and when you have shut your door, pray to your Father who is in the secret place; and your Father who sees in secret will reward you openly. And when you pray, do not use vain repetitions as the heathen do. For they think that they will be heard for their many words. Therefore, do not be like them. For your Father knows the things you have need of before you ask Him.* In this manner, therefore, pray: *Our Father in heaven, Hallowed be Your name. Your kingdom come. Your will be done on earth as it is in heaven. Give us this day our daily bread. And forgive us our debts, as we forgive our debtors. And do not lead us into temptation, but deliver us from the evil one. For Yours is the kingdom and the power and the glory forever. Amen. For if you forgive men their trespasses, your heavenly Father will also forgive you. But if you do not forgive men their trespasses, neither will your Father forgive your trespasses.* (Matthew 6:5–15; emphasis added)

Jesus has just told us how not to pray and how to pray. In the "how to pray" scenario, I want us to keep in mind some of the things we've gone over in this book that are evident in this prayer, such as

God seeing us as *one* people even though we are a many-membered man. So we pray *our* Father and not my Father and say give *us* and not give me. God wants us to think of ourselves as one. Then all being of the same mind and in one accord, we pray His will being done on earth as it is in heaven, then us not living by bread alone but God giving us our daily bread from His word as we go forth and learn to be quick to forgive so that we may also be forgiven and our prayers not be hindered. For it is all about Him! For His is the kingdom and the power and the glory, forever. Amen!

ABOUT THE AUTHOR

ANTONIO CRUMP, A former pastor and businessman, was born on a leap year in 1968 in Oklahoma City. However, it was his upbringing in the streets of Los Angeles, California, that shaped his unique perspective and life experiences.

At the age of eighteen, Tony got married to his beautiful wife, Theresa Crump. Together, they have been blessed with three children—Byron, Alisha, and Cherae Crump.

Tony's journey in faith began as a youth pastor and later as a pastor in Christianity, dedicating a decade of his life from 1993 to 2003 to guiding and uplifting others in their spiritual journeys.

In a surprising twist, Tony embarked on an unexpected path, spending the next two decades of his life as a truck driver from 2003 to 2023. His diverse life experiences allowed him to connect with people from all walks of life, fostering a deep understanding of the human condition and God's Word.